P9-ELG-603

SENSING
THE
SPIRIT

SPIRITUALITY AND THE CHRISTIAN LIFE SERIES
Richard H. Bell, *Editor*

SENSING
THE
SPIRIT

RICHARD H. BELL

THE WESTMINSTER PRESS
Philadelphia

Copyright © 1984 Richard H. Bell

All rights reserved—no part of this book may be reproduced in any form without permission in writing from the publisher, except by a reviewer who wishes to quote brief passages in connection with a review in magazine or newspaper.

Scripture quotations from the Revised Standard Version of the Bible are copyrighted 1946, 1952, © 1971, 1973 by the Division of Christian Education of the National Council of the Churches of Christ in the U.S.A. and are used by permission.

BOOK DESIGN BY ALICE DERR

First edition

Published by The Westminster Press®
Philadelphia, Pennsylvania

PRINTED IN THE UNITED STATES OF AMERICA
2 4 6 8 9 7 5 3 1

Library of Congress Cataloging in Publication Data

Bell, Richard H.
    Sensing the spirit.

    (Spirituality and the Christian life series)
    Bibliography: p.
    1. Spirituality. I. Title. II. Series.
BV4501.2.B3922 1984   248.4   84-5158
ISBN 0-664-24632-X (pbk.)

*With deep and abiding affection,
this book is dedicated to
my wife, Barbara,
my son, Jonathan,
my daughter, Rebecca,
and to all those ''bozos on the bus''
who were sojourners with me.*

CONTENTS

ACKNOWLEDGMENTS

This book is the result of a ten-year journey. I traveled through Great Britain and France, to East Africa, and across the United States, living and working in a dozen religious communities. I encountered many classical spiritual writers along the way and turned within myself to find clearer pathways of the spirit.

There are a score of my former students from The College of Wooster who will find themselves in these pages, and who gave me a modest opportunity to teach them while growing with them in mind and spirit.

The shape of the text itself was buffeted and refined by the critical eye of four friends who read an earlier draft with care. I owe gratitude to George Williamson, Granville, Ohio; Sharon Romich, Shreve, Ohio; Patricia Lull, Alpena, Michigan; and Ron Hustwit, Wooster, Ohio. Their suggestions improved this book immensely.

My family lovingly abandoned me to myself in the summer of 1983 to draft this book. Their patience and understanding go beyond measure.

I am indebted indirectly to the Dames of Oulton Abbey, Staffordshire, England, who I know have held me in their prayers for a decade, and whose Benedictine hospitality has been a reminder to me of genuine spiritual presence.

Finally, the President of The College of Wooster, Henry Copeland, and the Faculty Development Fund of the college were generous in support of my research and writing. Through the Mary Sager Sharp and William Dean Sager Endowment Fund, the college sponsored several conferences that were instrumental in the development of this whole series for The Westminster Press.

EDITOR'S INTRODUCTION

In 1609 Francis de Sales published a helpful book designed "to instruct those who live in town, within families, or at court, and by their state of life are obliged to live an ordinary life." It was, as he said, "a collection of bits of good advice stated in plain, intelligible words." The book, *Introduction to the Devout Life*, became a "spiritual classic." Although we will not claim that the books in this series will become spiritual classics, they are intended for a similar reader—one "obliged to live an ordinary life"—and they are written in "plain, intelligible words."

In terms of their subject matter, they share another point with Francis de Sales's book. He said about the Christian life that "a strong, resolute soul can live in the world without being infected by any of its moods." This was not an easy task then, nor is it now. But one of the goals of the Christian life is to free ourselves from circumstances that hinder love and service to God. When the apostle Paul spoke of having the "mind of Christ," he was asking that we not yield to the accidental features of this world; that we strive to free ourselves from being defined by the social, political, and economic principalities and powers of this world. A great effort of the spirit is needed to do this.

This series is intended to help its readers in this effort of the spirit. We call these books spiritual because they deal with how God's spirit intersects with the human spirit. They focus attention on the *Bible* as the principal source for hearing and understanding God's spirit and on the *self* as part of a living, worshiping, and struggling community of God's people in this world.

Living in the spirit first involves seeing and facing the many ways in which we forget God in our everyday life. It means having courage to suffer the wounds meted out by our world. Beyond these things, living in the spirit is an active disposition—*a formation* of faith and *a practice* of gratitude and compassion before God. Spiritual formation and practice come as we remember God and share his presence in us with others.

If no other books you have read lately have encouraged you to take hold of your self and your Christian life with courage and firmness, these books will. They will take you patiently through many identifiable thickets of human life and ask you when it was that you allowed God to speak to you, embrace you, and lead you. These books are intended to be traveling companions, guides to take you closer to the center of the Christian life, closer to the Bible, closer to yourself, and thus, it is hoped, closer to God.

This book, *Sensing the Spirit*, and its companions in the series, offer pathways for growing in the spirit. What may be only suggested in one book as a way of living as a Christian will be more richly developed in another. For example, the three disciplines of the spirit developed in this book—attention, refusal and renunciation, and loving God—are enriched by the notion of spirituality in worship and liturgy in Don Saliers' book *Worship and Spirituality*. Thus, this book and Saliers' could be read as complementary texts where the first emphasizes a personal spiritual journey and the second underscores the communal aspects of that journey through the life of the worshiping community of Christ. In the first chapter of William Stringfellow's book, *The Politics of Spirituality*, biblical spirituality is contrasted with the secular powers of this world. Here similar themes are struck with Part I of my book, though in a different mood. Stringfellow's book is more characteristically prophetic, while mine leads the reader more gently.

Between exploring the many ways in which we forget God and the disciplined steps for remembering him there lies a paradox. This paradox is central to my thesis. In God's absence we discover a yearning for his presence or all seems lost. To make explicit this yearning within us is the point of this book.

A special feature is the rich variety of spiritual writers used to augment the book's central themes. A personal pilgrimage is charted, and the reader is accompanied on the way by such writers as John of the Cross and Francis de Sales, François Fénelon and Roger Schutz, Simone Weil and Thomas Merton. With these writers and more, concrete practices for realizing God's presence in us are given to guide the reader. One paragraph in Chapter Nine sums up the end of this spiritual pilgrimage well:

> As we increase in our attention to this earthly life and practice acts of refusal to compensate for the errant moods of this world, we draw near to God. The consummating act is to regard God while we do these things and thus to call upon Christ to dwell in our acts. To live in this way is to perform the very sacrament of the Eucharist; it is to offer Christ as the bread of life to others and turn life itself into a living sacrament. To regard God and to love in Christ's way are to live one's life in *gratitude* and *compassion*.

Come, join us on our journeys.

PROLOGUE:
SPIRITUALITY

The American writer Flannery O'Connor, in *The Habit of Being* (p. 92), remarked to a friend:

> I am not a mystic and I do not lead a holy life. Not that I can claim any interesting or pleasurable sins . . . but I know all about the garden variety, pride, gluttony, envy and sloth, and what is more to the point, my virtues are as timid as my vices. I think sin occasionally brings one closer to God, but not habitual sin and not this petty kind that blocks every small good.

Few of us make claim to a "holy life." Nor do we think of ourselves as bad, though we do have vices (most likely of the garden variety) mixed with our virtues. Timid as our virtues may be, we do at times find courage to say no to our personal excesses, and we even object to hurtful acts when we see them imposed upon others. On balance we think of ourselves as good people.

Let us ask, however: Were we to make claim to a "holy life"—and not just a good one—how might we picture it? A pious image of Saint Francis? A striding, principled Mahatma Gandhi or Martin Luther King, Jr.? A humble, serving Mother Teresa of Calcutta? A martyred image of Saint Stephen or Dietrich Bonhoeffer? Images of a "holy life" may be justly varied, and many examples might do. But imaging such a life does not bring us closer to God. Most of us are not up to our heroes and heroines, and few of us aspire to be saints. So where do we turn to picture what some have called "the devout life"? Better still, where would we begin in setting out on such a path of devotion?

One place to start is to heighten our awareness of our vices. We might improve on our virtue by resisting all manner of evil around us. Awareness of our sin might bring us closer to God. Beyond this, however, a "holy life" requires holy assistance; it requires an active presence of God's spirit in our lives. Such an active presence of God's spirit, or living in the spirit, is often referred to as *spirituality*.

The very notion of spirituality, though, seems alien to Protestant Christians, perhaps less so to Roman or Orthodox believers. What is often underscored by Protestant believers is that our salvation is a matter of faith—an individual and personal matter. A "holy life," it might be said, is pinned to declarations of faith, unilateral declarations, declarations that bind God and believer by the saving grace of our Lord Jesus. Grace is that free gift of God mysteriously bestowed upon the world.

But even the Protestant tradition yokes this notion of grace by faith with some course of Christian perfection, with sanctifying deeds or works of the spirit—the purity of heart, patience, perseverance, self-control, love, joy, gentleness, kindness, and peace referred to by the apostle Paul (Gal. 5:22–23). God's grace and works of the spirit go hand in hand (James 2:14–16). What we call spirituality relates to how we live in this spirit and pursue a greater intimacy with the presence of God. Living in the spirit is finding ways to allow God's spirit to break gracefully into our lives.

There are, however, many diversions of a habitual, petty, and even larger kind that block God's spirit from breaking into our lives. There are scores of ways in which we forget God. It is these diversions and this forgetting that are the subject of the first half of this book. A discovery that I continually make in my own new beginnings and stumbling attempts at living in the spirit is this: As I become more aware of the ways I forget God, and as I enter into an active battle with these forgettings, the more I remember God. Furthermore, to sustain this remembering, I must discipline myself in specific ways to grow in God's spirit and continue to live in his presence. The second half of this book explores some specific disciplines of the spirit that help us remember God.

I am not a spiritual teacher, and any direction or advice offered in these pages comes from sources I have encountered along my own path and have found helpful in my own spiritual growth. What I have tried to do is to assemble reminders of how we forget God and how we might better remember him. I marshal insights from many who were (or are) spiritual teachers, so that the reader may be instructed by them. So the earthly guidance in these pages is from many who advanced far along a spiritual path and whose lives reflect an intimacy with the presence of God.

Spiritual presence is reflected in human lives; it comes through the witness of men and women in our world. Such a witness sometimes finds its way into words, and these words can be like seeds for us. We can plant them in our minds and hearts and turn and till them into the soil of our ordinary lives, however barren or fertile these lives may be. Among those who provide seeds for us are Augustine, John of the Cross, Francis de Sales, François Fénelon, John Bunyan, Jean Nicolas Grou, Søren Kierkegaard, Leo Tolstoy, Simone Weil, André Trocmé, Thomas Merton, Alexander Schmemann, Lanza del Vasto, and Roger Schutz. There are others, too, but these especially see the world in the light of Christ and, in their seeing, live by God's grace—freely, joyfully, and without fear of the wounds meted out by our world.

Among these teachers, one in particular, the French thinker Simone Weil, who André Gide said was "the most spiritual writer of this century," provides us with a pattern for *sensing the spirit*. This pattern moves from a clear awareness of the absence of God to an unencumbered embodiment of the presence of God. She understood fully the weaknesses of the human spirit without being discouraged or losing hope. She found a way of showing in her life a quiet, radical joy for living in this world through gratitude and compassion by the grace of the risen Lord.

It is my hope that something in these pages, with the help of many diverse teachers and with the particular spiritual pathway suggested, will enable us to sense the spirit more fully and joyfully and to combat the forces in this world that darken our lives and threaten to overwhelm us.

PART I

WAYS OF FORGETTING GOD

I should look upon every sin I have committed as a favor of God.

Simone Weil
Gravity and Grace

It is to the prodigals—to those who exhaust all their strength in pursuing what seems to them good and who, after their strength has failed, go on impotently desiring—that the memory of their Father's house comes back. If the son had lived economically he would never have thought of returning.

Simone Weil
Notebooks

CHAPTER ONE

OUR ORDINARY FORGETFULNESS

On May 10, 1983, upon receiving the Templeton Prize in Religion, Alexander Solzhenitsyn began his acceptance speech in the London Guildhall with these remarks:

> Over half a century ago, while I was still a child, I recall hearing a number of older people offer the following explanation for the great disasters that had befallen Russia: "Men have forgotten God; that's why all this has happened."
>
> Since then I have spent well-nigh 50 years working on the history of our revolution. . . .But if I were asked today to formulate as concisely as possible the main cause of the ruinous revolution that swallowed up some 60 million of our people, I could not put it more accurately than to repeat: "Men have forgotten God; that's why all this has happened."
>
> What is more, the events of the Russian revolution can only be understood now, at the end of the century, against the background of what has since occurred in the rest of the world. What emerges here is a process of universal significance. And if I were called upon to identify briefly the principal trait of the *entire* twentieth century, here too, I would be unable to find anything more precise and pithy than to repeat once again: "Men have forgotten God."
>
> (*The Times*, May 11, 1983; used by permission)

Solzhenitsyn went on to make grand and eloquent points about the loss of spirit in our age—"the flaw of a consciousness lacking all divine dimension," as he put it—swallowed up and blinded by "Godless communism" on the one hand and the rapacious appetites of "Western materialism" on the other. In the midst of apocalyptic imagery he said that "the noose on the neck of mankind draws tighter and more hopeless with every passing decade, and there seems to be no way out for anyone—neither nuclear, nor political, nor economic, nor ecological."

While what Solzhenitsyn says has a certain ring of truth to it, and I am disquieted by the thought that our entire century has forgotten God, I am at the same time just a bit uncertain about *my* role in this cosmic forgetfulness. I imagine that, like a thousand other Guildhall guests on that day, I would have squirmed in discomfort before such a prophetic address, sipped tea and talked of the great scourges of our time at the post-ceremony reception, and then gone quietly (though thoughtfully) home. In fact, one of those guests wrote me the following description of the event: "I now know what it must have been like to hear Amos or Jeremiah! Compelling authority to *hear* him . . . even if, with the 'top of one's mind,' one disagreed! Quite unforgettable."

But where are *we* in this great forgetfulness? I know what it means to forget my lunch or my umbrella, but forgetting God must be different. I cannot imagine a catastrophe befalling the world over my missing lunch or getting caught in a shower, but we do sense some dangers and larger discomforts in the idea of forgetting God. Would I, could I, really forget something so fundamental? God doesn't just fall out of my mind like my lunch may fall out of my hand, nor do I leave God behind like I do umbrellas. Besides, I am reminded of God in so many more ways than I am my lunch. Or am I? I don't actually forget my lunch that often, because my stomach reminds me of my hunger. But what will remind me of God? What comes to mind in answer to this question? I am reminded at table grace, on Sundays, in the religion section of *Time* and *Newsweek* . . . and at certain public ceremonies like Templeton awards. And then God comes to mind at those times when certain sympathies are called for—when a relative or friend dies, or some natural disaster occurs, or other human tragedies are played out before us in real life.

But am I not really telling myself more about how I forget God in the examples I just used to describe how I remember him? We would be hard pressed to defend the real efficacy that the thought of God has for us with this kind of remembering! It is hardly even as dependable as my hunger is in reminding me of my lunch. Maybe we have no real hunger for God, and we need something like that to remind us. But this might be part of Solzhenitsyn's point. And maybe we are misled by his talk of "Godless communism" and "Western materialism." Yes, it must be the case that my role in forgetting God is much less grandiose and cosmic; it is not like the entire twentieth century's having forgotten something but more like my lack of appetite, and the media always being there, and the mindless rhetoric of public officials droning on, and my busyness and constant lack of energy. It is to these ordinary kinds of forgetting and the paltry and episodic character of our remembering that we must address ourselves.

"Men have forgotten God"—and women too. This needs to be taken very seriously, and taken at the most mundane level of our forgetting. I will begin with some simple and ordinary ways in which we forget God and work toward some more difficult and less obvious aspects of our forgetting. In the end, however, I hope it becomes clear that in the very ordinariness of forgetting are the seeds that have grown into the extraordinariness of our present human condition.

All forms of our forgetting are a measure of our imperfection and our sinfulness. If we learn to recognize all these forms, then we position ourselves to have a real hunger for God.

Let us begin with a good biblical case about our forgetfulness. John in his Gospel recounts the following conversation between Jesus and Peter:

When they had finished breakfast, Jesus said to Simon Peter, "Simon, son of John, do you love me more than these?" He said to him, "Yes, Lord; you know that I love you." He said to him, "Feed my lambs." A second time he said to him, "Simon, son of John, do you love me?" He said to him, "Yes, Lord; you know that I love you." He said to him, "Tend my sheep." He said to him the third time, "Simon, son of John, do you love me?" Peter was grieved because he said to him the third time, "Do you love me?" And he said to him, "Lord, you know everything; you know that I love you." Jesus said to him, "Feed my sheep." (John 21:15–17)

Why does Jesus ask Peter three times to feed his sheep? Because he knows that Peter is likely to forget. And why is Peter likely to forget? Because it is a difficult job, and unlikely to bring either pleasure or reward to Peter. Peter is like most of us.

Jesus goes on to say to Peter:

Truly, truly, I say to you, when you were young, you girded yourself and walked where you would; but when you are old, you will stretch out your hands, and another will gird you and carry you where you do not wish to go. . . . "Follow me." (John 21:18–19)

Jesus reminds Peter and he reminds us that when we accept his ways and his will, our lives are no longer our own to do just as we wish—we are, as it were, under the control of God. It is, now, the spirit that is to guide us, and we must surrender to that guidance. Because the spirit may lead me where I would rather not go, I must prepare myself and accept whatever help will assist me on the journey.

We all want to know where we are going, and we also like to exercise control over our means of transport. Jesus guarantees neither, neither foreknowledge of where he may lead us nor what to expect of the path and the vehicle used in getting there. Because of this uncertainty, there are two easy escapes—two popular routes we could take—in response to his call to "follow": We could (1) *follow blindly*, stumbling along unaware of the implications of the journey, or (2) *make our own course*, devise our own destination and route there, then look back and place upon it a mildly religious interpretation—even call it a "Christian" way.

Few of us, if any, like the idea of blindly following anything; we are basically thinkers and planners, not robots or slaves. In the midst of our culture we are not often reminded of this point, but were we to find ourselves in another culture—one, say, with fewer freedoms and little prospect for being our own entrepreneurs—we might take notice. In a recent interview (*Harvard Divinity School Bulletin*, April–May 1983), Henri Nouwen says this about himself while living among the very poor in a South American nation: "I came to realize there that being a Western, Northern person, you always want to do something, you always want to have a plan. You see problems and you want to change something. We have a very structured kind of thinking." No one was going to mold Nouwen easily, nor was he going to settle patiently for no progress and no forward movement. To follow blindly or be forced to follow is not our cup of tea.

Nor would I think the second escape route the likely choice of most of us, though it is much more of a temptation to planners and doers. We would be more honest if, in making our own way, we would call it *ours* (thoroughly secular and contrived as it is) and not by a religious name. It could be embarrassing, if not idolatrous, to be caught in a deception (if not a lie) by making our own way and daring to call it Christian. Neither of these escapes will satisfy us; neither will allow God and Jesus or the spirit to grasp our unique personalities (who we are as "Western, Northern" persons); neither will allow us to recognize his Lordship and guidance and our genuine freedom and willing obedience.

A genuine Christian life—a life living in the spirit—is always to be found in the tension that comes from *hearing* God's Word, *sensing* what we are to do (and hard things they often are), and from our *free response* and *obedience* to God's address. The tension between God's address and our response points to both the need for devotion and the awareness of uncertainties: "Who me, Lord? You must be talking to someone else. *I* would rather not go there, but . . . if *you* will. . . ."

Living in the spirit is marked by a hunger to do God's will even though we tremble and recognize our limitations and uncertainties. God knows our frailties, our hardness of heart, our sin (especially our Western, Northern pride), and our uncertainty and thus gives us many reminders. God repeats similar messages in a variety of ways. He knows we need help and guidance to go down the difficult road he makes for us.

Even Peter, the Rock, had to be addressed over and over again, as if Jesus were saying, "Peter, I'm going to tell you something, but you are not going to get it: Feed my sheep." Why did Jesus suspect that Peter would not get the message, especially when Peter was aware that Jesus knew everything? Jesus knew Peter loved him. It is *precisely because* God and Jesus know us so well that we must be reminded over and over again. Our forgetfulness is endemic when we think our interests are not served. God and Jesus know that where we are asked to go is usually not where we would choose to go! And if we are not reminded, we will seldom, or at best only reluctantly, follow.

There is a sense in which we can understand Peter's hurt and sadness when Jesus did not accept his initial response: "Yes, Lord; you know that I love you." Peter wanted to follow Jesus, but he was not clear what that would entail. And Jesus knew this. So both his command to "feed my sheep" and the response of Peter's love had to be repeated. In the repetition, Peter's faith, his sense of the address, was strengthened and his call clarified.

We too must have our calls clarified, presented to us more than once, so that we can take courage in our responses to the risks they may demand of us. The Bible is a *living word* and demands we question it, wrestle with it, love it, respond to it, listen to it—all this in a way we would in a genuine conversation with our closest friend, our spouse, our child, our lover. Hearing the Word, sensing the address of the Bible to us, we must realize that we may be asked to go where we would rather not go.

Let me return for a moment to this notion of our being Western, Northern persons, as Henri Nouwen put it. While recently teaching an adult church school class, I asked each of some fifty upwardly mobile Presbyterians to select one or more of the following as recognizable reasons for not reading their Bible regularly:

(a) Too busy.
(b) Too afraid of what I might find.
(c) Have a poor memory for foreign names and long genealogies.
(d) Too slow a reader.
(e) Untutored in the critical and literary genres of the Bible.
(f) Think I've already read it.
(g) Think it's not contemporary or "relevant."
(h) Count on my pastor to do the reading and interpreting for me.
(i) Forget where I put it.

After thinking about the list for a while, a young man remarked, "You left a reason off the list that struck me when I finished reading it." "What's that?" I asked. He said, "(j) All of the above!"

Although we might find ourselves agreeing with such items on the list, none—except for (b), our fear of facing something we would rather avoid—is a very substantial reason for not taking the Bible more seriously. Each is a temporary roadblock, set up for no other reason than not stopping to take time to listen to, and perhaps discuss, what God may have to say to us. All are symptoms of simple avoidance, and thus they function to *void* the prospect of hearing God's Word.

The reasons listed, however, do say a great deal about our daily preoccupations as Western, Northern persons. To such persons, conversing with God's Word is unnecessary; it simply does not matter on the scale of things that "matter":

achievement, power, status, fashion, running in the fast lane, and personal aesthetic pleasures. These things that matter are identifiable with a certain level of social and economic affluence—the level we enjoy—and have little to do with matters of fundamental importance to basic human needs or wants.

God's Word addresses basic human needs and wants, but the life we have created for ourselves has substantially hidden or glossed over such basic needs and wants. The famous Swiss psychoanalyst C. G. Jung wrote, over a generation ago:

> Whether from an intellectual, moral or aesthetic point of view, the undercurrents of the psychic life of the West are an uninviting picture. We have built a monumental world about us, and we have slaved for it with unequalled energy. But it is so imposing because we spent upon the outside all that is imposing on our natures—and what we find when we look within must necessarily be as it is, shabby and insufficient. (Quoted in Douglas V. Steere, *On Beginning from Within*, p. 9)

The more energy spent on the outside, the more the spirit withers within. And we seem only to be shoring up the outside, insulating our hollowness from extreme vulnerability. We will not stop and pay heed, or turn a reflective glance upon our shabbiness. Instead, our psychic undercurrents have this forward movement; progress is our watchword and success our guide.

It is not my intention to lead you toward how we might have a personal conversation with biblical texts—that is the subject of an earlier book in this series (H. A. Nielsen, *The Bible—As If for the First Time*)—but I am concerned about barriers to hearing God, to sensing the spirit, and about this forgetfulness so characteristic of our earthly life. I am concerned about the diversions and deceptions we create for ourselves that keep us from discerning God's presence to us.

There is a connected matter to our avoiding and thus forgetting God. Today we are totally preoccupied with our own words. Our words readily displace God's Word, our political rhetoric has neutralized our moral seriousness, and, simply, our incessant talking fills every space in our lives in order to avoid encounters with silence and with ourselves. We do not wish to face up to what we might find within.

Our verbal fluency and communications mania have become one (if not *the*) major diversion we employ to keep from sensing the spirit. Words, being processed in every conceivable manner—in speech and in type, in BASIC, COBAL, and PASCAL; disseminated in print, on video and audio, and stored on microchip in RAM and ROM ready for recall at a rate of thousands of words per minute—all serve as diversions to needs of the spirit. Words have made virtually every kind of knowledge accessible, but our words have neither improved our moral life nor brought us closer to God. In spite of our millennia of verbal assaults on the supernatural and our current capacity to store billions of bytes of data in near perpetuity, the spirit remains ineffable.

Using words to deceive ourselves about our moral and political purposes and our religious aspirations is not something new to our generation, or even to our age. Modern sensibilities have not improved upon this fifth-century testimony of Augustine (354–430), student of rhetoric, master of speech and argument, who, despite his talents, fell further from God and the spirit the more he embraced his rhetorical successes. We can see ourselves in his own *Confessions* (p. 39):

> O God, alone in majesty, high in the silence of heaven, unseen by man! We can see how your unremitting justice punishes unlawful ambition with blindness, for a man who longs for fame as a fine speaker will stand up before a human judge, surrounded by a human audience, and lash his opponent with malicious invective, taking the greatest care not to say "uman" instead of "human" by a slip of the tongue, and yet the thought that the frenzy in his own mind may condemn a human being to death disturbs him not at all.

Augustine's remark is hauntingly indicting. "Ambition with blindness," "fame," the pressures for fine speaking and the merits of self-assertion; the verbal "invective," "malicious" without a thought of the harm it may do. We are taught these things in our schools and praised for our successes. To verbally condemn another human being disturbs us not at all.

Another example of this tempting power of words to cast a spell over us is found in the classic of John Bunyan (1628–1688), *The Pilgrim's Progress*. In one encounter Bunyan shows how Faithful was beguiled by Talkative before having his eyes opened by Christian. Bunyan writes (p. 82):

> How Talkative at first lifts up his plumes!
> How bravely doth he speak! How he presumes
> To drive down all before him! But so soon
> As Faithful talks of heart-work, like the moon
> That's past the full, into the wane he goes.
> And so will all but he that heartwork knows.

Today our verbal plumage is great; we presume to drive down our adversaries, and no waning is in sight. In this passage Bunyan has introduced a term that will bear some importance for us later on—"heartwork." In Bunyan's heartwork we have a clue to where we might turn to notice God's address to us, to sense the presence of the spirit in us.

It is heartwork, not our words, that unveils the spirit. A formed spirituality knows this, but few in our time do. Of Talkative, Christian says (pp. 75, 77):

> "Religion hath no place in his heart, or house, or conversation; all he hath lieth in his tongue; and his religion is to make a noise therewith. . . . Talking is not sufficient to prove that fruit is indeed in the heart and life."

We all know a Talkative, one who fills our airwaves, even our pulpits. Theologians and politicians and gurus all have this special skill. But heartwork is too often missing; it has no place in Talkative's "heart or house or conversation."

Conversation, here, implies that there is dialogue and exchange in human life—listening and responding, not turning away like the waning of the moon.

Finally, wherein does the real danger of our words lie? It lies in *signaling* great events and great actions without requiring that we *do* anything about such events and actions. Our words often signal finality with no further expectations involved.

My friend in London, who disagreed in mind but found Solzhenitsyn's words "quite unforgettable," and all those we know who go quietly home recall to mind this parable from the nineteenth-century Danish thinker Søren Kierkegaard:

> A revolutionary age is an age of action; ours is the age of advertisement and publicity. Nothing ever happens but there is immediate publicity everywhere. In the present age a rebellion is, of all things, the most unthinkable. Such an expression of strength would seem ridiculous to the calculating intelligence of our times. On the other hand a political virtuoso might bring off a feat almost as remarkable. He might write a manifesto suggesting a general assembly at which people should decide upon a rebellion, and it would be so carefully worded that even the censor would let it pass. At the meeting itself he would be able to create the impression that his audience had rebelled, after which they would all go quietly home—having spent a very pleasant evening. (*Parables of Kierkegaard*, p. 75)

We are all a bit "talkative," but sometimes we have something to say for which someone stops to listen. We are not all drones. Sometimes, even, we may pick up the Bible and take comfort in something we read, or be surprised that it seems to address us directly, to the point of our concerns. But then think how we are more often swayed by Kierkegaard's "political virtuoso" or deceived by those with "calculating intelligence," even by a general assembly gathered, where we decide on what seems only short of rebellion and then "go quietly home." Even though we may dis-

agree with the top of our minds, as my friend did with Solzhenitsyn, we may only be thoughtfully stirred; that is more
like how we live in this world. To be thoughtfully stirred,
however, or to rebel only by proxy, is to leave out heartwork.

CHAPTER TWO

DECEPTION, SELF-IMPORTANCE, AND SELF-INTEREST

A great thinker of our century, Ludwig Wittgenstein (1889–1951), remarked, "Nothing is so difficult as not deceiving oneself." We are all aware of the fact that we *do* deceive ourselves, but as he recognized the *hard* thing is *not* to do so.

We continually deceive ourselves and, in so doing, forget God in many things—especially in our concern for self-importance. The daily exercises of power in our life—again, those things that we say matter to us: achievements, status, our fashions, words, rhetorical successes—all remind us of our need for self-importance. But because power in this earthly life is the instrument by which deception grows and by which we come to accept clichés like "more (or bigger) is better" or "might makes right," we quickly lose a sense of proportion and perspective on ourselves and our achievements.

There is something illusory about self-importance. It pretends to enable us to exercise control over things, but we know all along our control is fragile at best and futile at worst. One of the grand illusions of self-importance is thinking that we are more advanced than we are. In this our opinions take on inflated importance. We can take some credit for human advances, but such credit as we do take must be quickly qualified by human failures as well. What we cannot do is tie our advances to our wealth and power. This heightens the illusion of our importance and edges the power of God further from our mind and heart. We have all heard the adage, "Power corrupts, and absolute power corrupts absolutely." When we place this worldly power next to God's power, the roots of human sin are unearthed.

In our advanced opinions, we corrupt not only ourselves but also those on whom we impose our values. If we note again how inflated values gloss over basic human needs and wants because such needs and wants are taken for granted, then by imposing the values we hold on people who cannot assume that such needs and wants will be fulfilled—the poor, hungry, and malnourished, the oppressed, and those enslaved by tyranny—we breed their envy. We lead them to think that they are nothing and we are something by virtue of our wealth and power. It also moves us further away from a recognition that human needs are fundamental to the spirit. Such basic needs point to our limits and dependencies, to the banalities of ordinary human life.

We should not deny that *we are something*, or that human beings as God's crowning creation have no importance in the world community, but our importance should not be measured by our worldly power and riches. To do so is at the very heart of sin; it is the denial of the power of God. The sin attached to self-importance goes beyond simple platitudes of self-reliant behavior; it moves toward self-aggrandizement and arrogance, to sovereignty, and finally to an idolatrous self-adulation. What is more contrary to a life governed by God's spirit than a life spent always taking matters into one's own hands?

To be firm and strong, to persevere, to be good stewards and use our talents prudently—all these are human virtues. Furthermore, they are blessed by God and should be practiced freely. There is a difference, however, as to who governs the exercise of these virtues. In the Christian life these virtues are always to be understood and used under the guidance of God. Confidence in one's own talents, for example, exercised under God's guidance is essential to the Christian life, but confidence exercised without such guidance, with misplaced self-importance, easily turns to conceit.

We are called to be strong in the Lord, to persevere in the face of adversity as well as in times of plenty, knowing that God will take up our burdens. In the end, for the Christian life, anxieties and suffering, bounty and blessing, talents and knowledge are to be submitted to the guidance of God and not to the exercises of power available to us. All such means are temptations, forms of deception that lead us away from God and encourage a certain sovereign self-reliance. The wisdom of Solomon says it simply:

> May God grant that I speak with judgment
> and have thoughts worthy of what I have received,
> for he is the guide even of wisdom,
> and the corrector of the wise.
> For both we and our words are in his hand,
> as are all understanding and skill in crafts.
>
> (Wisdom 7:15–16)

We often hear from very conservative Christian circles that "humanism" has taken hold of our lives and that Christianity must fight it at every turn. The truth in this charge is that in our being human is our capacity to sin, and as we sin we move farther from God. But the danger in such a sweeping condemnation of all things humanly grounded is the belief that a gloss or veneer of "Christian talk" (being a Talkative) will override our very human qualities. We *have* in so many ways abandoned God in our world. Those who decry our secularism have seen things rightly. But our secular abandonment of God has been done by individually and incrementally taking charge of our own destinies. And the irony and self-deceit in the too-conservative attack on "humanists" is a new cry to take charge—take charge of schools, of morality, of politics—all of which plays into the worldly power game and is itself a new deception and manifestation of self-importance or pride. Too often we want to be managers; we want to manage our own affairs. But how do we know when our own affairs are not someone else's as well?

Our world is an interconnected one, not a world of discrete persons and discrete affairs.

What can countervail such a tendency to want to be in charge, such insidiously incremental growth in pride? If in our daily social life, in our rituals of power, we abandon God for our self-importance, how can we restore a climate whereby God's presence becomes more apparent to us? The hard thing here is not deceiving ourselves; the hard thing here is getting a fix on such deception so that we can look elsewhere to avoid its worst forms.

Here is a down-to-earth example from a parent who saw "the beast" in this self-important power game and called a halt to it. In the *Newsweek* "My Turn" column of March 28, 1983, speaking of the difficulties in raising children, Francine Klagsbrun declared that "if I had to choose between excessive self-sacrifice and excessive self-fulfillment as parental goals, I would stick to self-sacrifice." Such self-sacrifice is a sign of care and commitment, not to mention a virtue requiring strength of character, the paradigm of what the author calls the classic "Jewish mother." Does such advice apply only to parents? Of course not. This good advice focuses rather on an aspect of this deep sin of our time—this pride—now in the name of "excessive self-fulfillment."

But, like self-importance, why should we call self-fulfillment sin? How is pride caught up with "excessive self-fulfillment"? Francine Klagsbrun sees it rightly. We abandon our children in the pursuit of our self-interests and pleasures—"extremists," as she says, "of the remote, 'Ordinary People' school," where everyone pursues individual paths to fulfill individual potential.

Francine Klagsbrun is not so much railing at those selfish self-realizers as she is pointing to the fact that we may have misunderstood self-fulfillment altogether. Maybe it comes with sacrifice—that, at least, is strongly suggested in the Bible: both testaments. With the care of a child goes a great deal of sacrifice. There is something fundamentally askew in thinking that sweating over chicken soup is less self-fulfilling than sweating over one's job.

So that you won't think I am suggesting women should return to the kitchen, let me suggest some different ways of understanding self-fulfillment and sacrifice. Saying that self-fulfillment may come with sacrifice is not to imply that sacrificial behavior is passive and submissive to oppressive social traditions. I would argue, for example, that parents who are self-giving are stronger in spirit and more likely to sustain the love and nurture of their children than are world-dependent parents.

Self-fulfillment attached with sacrifice rather than self-assertion first requires that one have possession of one's self. Only then can a self be sacrificed to another. There are those who, by virtue of being victims of oppression, have not been allowed to possess themselves. Such persons need first to gain self-confidence, perhaps even strength to be assertive, in order to remember and recall the hope in their hearts that can fulfill their nature. The notion of self-possession as an expression of human worth will be developed in Chapters Seven and Eight in relationship to remembering God. There we will find the need to declare a certain spiritual independence under God's rule, rather than a sovereign self-reliance under worldly rule.

We are talking about two basic human orientations: the one, self-sacrificial behavior, and the other, self-fulfillment behavior. On the surface they appear incompatible. *Self-sacrificial behavior* requires giving up something and seems to depend on some outside guidance or encouragement for constant renewal. Although it is not altogether unnatural, self-sacrificial behavior runs counter to some strong self-interested passions and requires a humility sufficient to call upon others for help. *Self-fulfillment behavior* is a strong inner orientation, driven by personal appetites and pleasures; it is a kind of self-gyroscopic behavior, a turning around oneself and continually orienting one's actions toward self-centering interests. It is conditioned by the demand to become self-sufficient.

Self-fulfillment behavior, as we have come to know it, focuses a lot of attention on the autonomous individual and the ability to be self-assertive. Techniques and schools have developed under the general rubric of "human potential movements" to encourage self-fulfilling behavior. These have both secular and sacred forms: transcendental meditation (TM) and transactional analysis (TA) and the power of "positive" and "possibility" thinking—to mention only four techniques for such self-realization. Each technique detracts from our awareness of any need for guidance from outside ourselves. We are not to look for help from others—parents, children, friends, neighbors, or brothers and sisters in the faith—least of all from God or the Holy Spirit. We abandon the need to account to anyone other than our self.

When we so abandon others and God, we fall into greater dependence on self-reliant behavior, and this behavior requires tremendous energy reserves. With such energy pouring out of each individual's store, we experience an inflation of our human achievements—that is, we begin to think very highly of what we do. With such inflation of human achievements, we also experience increased anxiety and stress because we fall behind in the race to keep up with what we see others to be achieving. This we call, not so affectionately, the "rat race." We all seem to be in it and see no way out. The difficulty is in not deceiving oneself.

The deception in our concern for self-importance or the popular varieties of self-fulfillment—this subtle but dominant form of human pride—is just one way that we forget, and thus abandon, God. This deceptive pride is an obstacle in sensing the spirit. Forms of human pride exalt us and blur human limits; they promote mistaken beliefs in our own strength and place us into the position of measuring ourselves by inflated human standards.

The point here is to gain possession of one's self as a worthy child of God, to break away from the oppressive forces that belittle our personal worth and dignity and put us in the unhappy position of generating new psychological gimmicks to restore our fallen health.

Lanza del Vasto (1901–), founder of the French community of the Ark, based upon Christian-Gandhian principles, speaks of this pride as Hindrance, an "order of inner enslavement," and says, in *Principles and Precepts of the Return to the Obvious* (p.89):

If you want to escape from Hindrance, do not try to augment your power in proportion to the covetousness of pride and ambition, for Hindrance will augment in like measure.

Reduce your desires to your needs, your ambition to surpassing yourself and your pride to considering the dignity of your essence.

The dignity of our essence, according to our biblical heritage, is to love and to serve God; in the words of one survivor of the Jewish Holocaust, we are on earth "to be in God's service, to do God's bidding."

There is still another deception that focuses more specifically on an aspect of our self-interest. This is a deception in our moral life called *ethical relativism*. It says "to each his own." In ethical relativism each person is sovereign, providing individual boundaries for what is right and what is wrong. This is the ancient Protagorean maxim that I am the measure of all things; that what I prefer and what gives me pleasure is OK. This view has a firm hold in our culture. It is believed that an individual who fails to assert sovereignty and self-interest is benignly swallowed up in the prevailing order dictated by various bureaucracies.

Take, for example, two recent ethical trends in our society, the "new morality" and the "moral majority." Although each pretends to be ideologically at odds with the other, they are simply two sides of a similar moral coin. With the "new morality," which is characteristically associated with a certain libertarian view—each to one's own and "do your own thing"—we see the outcropping of individual sovereignty against control of the benign bureaucracy. In its most radical form, hippie advocate of the "new morality" Jerry Rubin cried, *"Do it!"*—and "it" meant anything that *you* thought was right or that made *you* feel good. With the "moral majority," the cry is *"Don't do it!"* This, too, is a reaction against the benign bureaucracy controlling our individuality. "It," for this group, is any outside interference with my freedom. So both the "new morality" and the "moral majority" are radical expressions of individuality.

Where the two movements have internal coherence is when they focus energies around a cause. With the "new morality" it may be anticensorship, free choice, human rights, or peace-and-justice issues; for the "moral majority" the causes may be antipornography, antiabortion, or prayer in schools. Both call for noninterference with their local and individual affairs; both want to assert their sovereignty as individuals; neither wishes to be told what to do. Yet, with all these likenesses, neither wishes to appeal to any common rational grounds for moral agreement. Members of one group point to human nature or natural rights and interpret that to suit their interests, while members of the other group point to divine authority or Scripture and interpret that to suit *their* interests. What both appeals come down to are simply justifications of the relative actions of a group of persons that serve their particular and very local self-interests.

Were I to place the typical college student, whom I teach, before an advocate of these views—say, the old Jerry Rubin on one side and Jerry Falwell on the other—and even if the student was inclined to one Jerry or the other, or to neither, and I asked, "Which Jerry is right and whom should I condemn?" they would probably respond, "Well, who's to judge?" Who's to judge? That, of course, is the coup de grace of ethical relativism. Even though the relativists believe that there are no mutual grounds for moral judgment, their refusal to judge is the ultimate expression of indifference; it is the soul of moral paralysis that this so-called moral pluralism breeds. "I may disagree with what you do, but it is your right to do it!" The two Jerrys' disagreement may be on a matter of little consequence, but taken a step further, a person confronted with some monstrous political injustice, for instance, may feel no confidence in protesting or fighting against it because, as he or she says, "Who's to judge? It's only my feelings against theirs." The tragedy of this view is that it is much like a mindless game of Russian roulette; lurking in one of those chambers not noted by our moral action or inaction may be a different Jerry or a tyrannous bureaucracy that is not so benign.

What has happened with this new pluralism and relativism is that we have been forced to reinvent morality; to make our own way and call it ethical or religious. This, too, serves our self-interest, but it goes only so far as we see conflicts arise all around us. The stock response to such conflicts is to avoid them rather than resolve them by some mutual yielding or reciprocity, or by finding a common ground upon which we might agree. We avoid the conflict altogether and hope it will go away. It usually does not, of course. All this relativizing of moral outlooks has bred a deep skepticism in us and keeps us from seeing and acting with conviction. Although we say we still see good and evil in the world and that we know a hurtful act from a helpful one, what we have lost is the sense of *how to act* in terms of a good or an evil we do see. Solzhenitsyn in his Templeton address said it this way: "The concepts of good and evil have been ridiculed for several centuries; banished from common use, they have been replaced by political or class considerations of short-lived value."

Novelist and philosopher William Gass makes this point quite simply (p. 240):

> Ethics, I wish to say, is about something, and in the rush to establish principles . . . and to discover "laws," those lovely things and honored people, those vile seducers and ruddy villains our principles and laws are supposed to be based upon and our ethical theories to be about, are overlooked and forgotten.

What we are trying to do here is to not overlook and forget such "vile seducers and ruddy villains," so that we might see the degree to which God has become absent from our lives. Then, perhaps, we can begin to take heart in "those lovely things and honored people."

CHAPTER THREE

PROTECTION AGAINST HARM AND DOING HARM

Our daily preoccupations as Western, Northern people and our pride of self-importance and self-fulfillment are not the only reason for our forgetting God. Because there is so much in the world that seems to hurt us, we build up earthly defenses for protection. What could be more natural and normal than protecting ourselves against harm? But here, too, is a subtle deception, for in our rush for protection in an increasingly hostile world, we close ourselves off from others; we forget to trust others; we forget to trust God; we insulate ourselves from help. In turn, we find it more difficult to offer help to others, for *they* have become insulated from *us*. It is hard not to protect ourselves.

In protection against harm we easily abandon God, we forget others, and in this forgetting we turn away from Christ as well. What we do for others, Christ said, is precisely what we do for him, and what we fail to do for others we fail to do for him also. The ways we turn away from Christ are often masked in our ordinary commerce. And because we do not see the connection between such commerce and our faith, the deception goes unnoticed.

Our global economy, for example, is in great imbalance between rich and poor. Tensions from the inequities begin to press urgently upon each human being. Those who are poor, and are either exploited or believe themselves to be unjustly neglected, harbor a growing resentment and mistrust of those who have wealth and power. The poor make up over two thirds of the world's people. Those who have wealth are following the conservative instinct to shore up and protect what they have, out of growing fear. And this, oddly enough, is in the face of growing evidence of the necessity for greater global economic interdependence. Those who have wealth—and we are among them—are fewer than one third of the world's people. Such a climate heightens world tensions and further isolates the individual parts of the human family. It divides northern from southern hemisphere; it divides eastern from western block nations; it divides the advantaged from the disadvantaged within every country.

What is being played out on the global stage has its implications for the home theater as well. Rapid inflation fuels the frustrations of every buyer and promotes an attitude of "better get it now or not get it at all." This is a brutal form of selfishness. The consumer spiral of getting and spending becomes a way of life and a hazard to health and wholeness, because it zeroes in on *my wants*, often at the cost of *others' needs*. The only protection we seem to have is to hedge against inflation by a greater self-concern. The needs and interests of others come second to our own, if they come at all. This economic self-concern hurts us. Despite some hopeful rays of light from those who follow the "small is beautiful" manuals, we are generally witnessing an increase in personal anxiety. As our self-protectiveness increases, our social concern decreases. As social concern decreases, our global well-being declines. As we try harder to avoid personal defeats, we become more and more insulated, socially and economically; we are drawn deeper into a spiral of self-concern and self-isolation; we distance ourselves from the central Christian and human concept of *community*.

Another way of construing this is to note its ordinariness—to see it as an extension of our natural desires and self-interest (which is, of course, how Adam Smith got to his points about economics). This way it may appear more benign than in its economic and social forms. Philosophers such as Aristotle and Augustine saw self-interest as a natural passion, part of our animal nature. A contemporary philosopher, Diogenes Allen, has called this "the route of desire"—a route that in itself can lead to either a full and happy life or an empty one. In our ordinary pursuit of happiness the objects of our desire determine to a large extent the outcome of our life. And regardless of the objects we choose, "we never seem satisfied with what we possess or achieve; we are restless and crave what is novel." Allen, in *The Traces of God* (pp. 14f.), points us to this image of Plato:

> We are like leaky vessels. It is as though we were containers into which we keep pouring things, but we never get filled up because there is a hole in each container and something is always leaking out. So we spend our lives trying to attain fullness, satisfaction, and completeness, and yet we never do. We go on thinking that if only we had just a bit more, then we would be satisfied; if we had something else, then our potential would be realized, our happiness assured, and our fulfillment achieved. . . .
>
> Our desires are for things we can *imagine*, and they push us on and on relentlessly from one thing to another, seeking in one place after another to satisfy that hunger for fullness. Some people consume everything in sight; others arrange their lives more prudently so as to gain the maximum of satisfaction, and exercise their imagination on goals they would love to attain. All this holds us firmly fixed to the ground as powerfully as the force of gravity holds our bodies to the earth. We love this world and everything in it that promises to give us fullness of life.

To desire God, however, is quite another matter. As we find our way in this earthly life, we have little to go on that tangibly and strikingly reminds us of God. Our imaginings are grounded—and God, by and large, is not grounded in the same ways as the goods and people and successes we desire.

To turn our desires to God, says Allen, we must first

"withhold" ourselves from our preoccupation with earthly things. "It begins with our refusal to give our love to anything of this world, our decision to hold back, to renounce, because we realize that there is nothing in this world that can fully satisfy us" (p. 15). Furthermore, such a refusal hurts us; it requires some sacrifices and thus runs counter to what we have earlier identified as self-fulfilling behavior.

Perhaps the most vivid picture in literature we have of the desperate end of this route of desire when oriented toward worldly happiness is in Leo Tolstoy's *The Death of Ivan Ilych*. Ivan Ilych has deceived himself throughout his life, and it is not until he is faced with a terrible death that he can let go of his human desires and be still. It is then that these thoughts surface (p. 152):

> "Maybe I did not live as I ought to have done," it suddenly occurred to him. "But how could that be, when I did everything properly?" And again he questioned: "What if my whole life has really been wrong?"

Such a dramatic realization—that one's "whole life has really been wrong"! With such a realization comes great pain. But even to realize that some *small thing* in our life might be wrong—some relationship, some nagging detail in our past, a missed opportunity to help, or a friend mistreated—can be agonizing. Such realizations are, as they were for Ivan Ilych, a form of spiritual death, a dying to the spirit in order to be reborn to God's presence; they require a denial of our self-deceptive claim to "right" living.

It is, however, such self-sacrificial behavior, such refusal, that checks our human desires and creates the possibility for God's presence to make itself known to us. Acts of refusal, of renunciation, of sacrifice are difficult, to be sure, but they also remind us of how God is absent from our lives when each moment is taken up by our habit of consuming.

In the end there is little we can do to ensure against social and economic calamity, or against the insatiable aspects of our human nature. The world economy, the social fate of our world, our animal natures move by forces we can neither fully comprehend nor effectively control. All our protective castles and kingdoms may be no more than houses of cards. This points to one kind of vulnerability that humans possess despite our protective instincts. There are more than enough lessons in history and in daily life to keep us from thinking we are invulnerable to the changing tides of this earthly life.

To call these economic and social liabilities to mind, as well as this route of our avaricious desires, is enough to remind us of a penultimate vulnerability that goes along with the ultimate vulnerability of human life: the vulnerability of death. Our economic and social vulnerabilities need to be placed alongside this other human vulnerability. Only then can we see our earthly pursuits for what they are: temporary and relatively short-lived, unsatisfying and unfulfilling. When we ask ourselves such an important question as "What do we want for our heirs, our children, in this world?" the answer must be sought in terms of the specific local and global environments in which they will live. What are they to look like? How long can we deceive ourselves into thinking there will always be more, always be a relative state of peace, always be a turn of events that will avoid a great disaster? When the question is asked about our children and heirs, it must be answered in terms of our and their happiness, and this latter point about our happiness has to do with how we live in the face of the ultimate vulnerability, our death.

When it comes to being harmed and understanding the harm—both in economic and social ways and in the harsher manner of our physical suffering even to death—we can continually learn from returning to the story of Job. This book in Scripture we often avoid reading because it seems either too harsh or too difficult for our understanding.

Some of the difficulty of Job was removed for me by Rabbi Harold Kushner's book *When Bad Things Happen to Good People*. Kushner helped me to see that what Job wanted most was not theological answers but some help from friends in facing what was happening to him and which, to anyone's eyes, was dreadfully unfair. What helped bring Ivan Ilych to the realization of the wrongness of his life in spite of its being "properly" lived was the fact that his servant, Gerasim, held his hand when he suffered most, while his family felt inconvenienced by his long illness. Kushner also helps us to see that there is really no protection against some kinds of harm and suffering; there is only finding a way to deal with it by being helped and helping others. I want to share Kushner's thoughts on these two points: what Job needed most, and how we can think of God in the context of human harm and suffering.

First, about what Job needed most, Kushner writes, "Job asked questions about God, but he did not need lessons in theology. He needed sympathy and compassion and the reassurance that he was a good person and cherished friend." We do not know why some things happen. We ask, Why am I being hurt? but the biblical answer cannot be because I either deserved the punishment or needed a plague to muster my courage. Kushner goes on to say that a sick and dying neighbor, like Job, "needs help in keeping his mind and spirit strong, so that he can look forward to a future in which he will be able to think and plan and decide" (p. 68). The biblical faith tells us that God gives us strength and courage to face adversity and our human vulnerabilities, our pain and the fear of death. It is this encouragement that is needed during times of trial.

What Job got, however, were theological explanations, which was no help. In the end, Job faces up to it himself and, through an agonizing self-affliction and spiritual death, yields to God. Job had little help from others. But what understanding of God does Job help us with? Well, theologically, it won't do to hold God responsible even though God seems to be bringing about the harm. What we do see in Job's reaction is his instinctive sense of its unfairness, his outrage and indignation. Kushner notes that we could look at this unfairness and declare, "There is no God." Or we could ask, "Where did Job get his sense of the unfairness of it all?" Kushner poses this very important question for us (p. 142): "Where do I get my sense of outrage and indignation, my instinctive response of sympathy when I read in the pa-per about a total stranger who has been hurt by life?" In a series of rhetorical questions, he answers:

> Don't I get these things from God? Doesn't He plant in me a little bit of His own divine outrage at injustice and oppression, just as He did for the prophets of the Bible? Isn't my feeling of compassion for the afflicted just a reflection of the compassion He feels when He sees the suffering of His creatures?

It is a paradox that when God seems absent and we are angry and indignant, we may be experiencing a flicker of God's presence working through us.

Earlier in his book, Kushner makes a similar point by turning our attention to the concept of justice rather than power in relation to God and evil. In dealing with the theodicy question, theologians stumble on the notion of God's power, as did Job and his friends who sought an explanation to his plight. If, however, we think of God as a God of justice and not predominantly of power, we can think of him as being on our side when we suffer, when bad things happen to us. As nature is indifferent to the righteous and the unrighteous—to good and bad people—so God, too, can be on our side with compassion when we do suffer. It is not a matter of reward and punishment. We can, as Kushner suggests (p. 45),

> recognize our anger at life's unfairness, our instinctive compassion at seeing people suffer, as coming from God who teaches us to be angry at injustice and to feel compassion for the afflicted. Instead of feeling that we are opposed to God, we can feel that our indignation is God's anger at unfairness working through us, that when we cry out, we are still on God's side, and He is still on ours.

When Kushner carries this over to the evils that we humans do each other, he says of the treatment of Jews by the Nazis, "I have to believe that the Holocaust was at least as much of an offense to God's moral order as it is to mine, or how can I respect God as a source of moral guidance?" (p. 82). Kushner's remarks on why the Holocaust happened and how God fits into it are worth quoting at length (pp. 84f.):

> The Holocaust happened because Hitler was a demented evil genius who chose to do harm on a massive scale. But he did not cause it alone. Hitler was only one man, and even his ability to do evil was limited. The Holocaust happened because thousands of others could be persuaded to join him in his madness, and millions of others permitted themselves to be frightened or shamed into cooperating. It happened because angry, frustrated people were willing to vent their anger and frustration on innocent victims as soon as someone encouraged them to do so. It happened because Hitler was able to persuade lawyers to forget their commitment to justice and doctors to violate their oaths. And it happened because democratic governments were unwilling to summon their people to stand up to Hitler as long as their own interests were not yet at stake.
>
> Where was God while all this was going on? . . . I have to believe, with Dorothee Soelle, that He was with the victims, and not with the murderers, but that He does not control man's choosing between good and evil. I have to believe that the tears and prayers of the victims aroused God's compassion, but having given Man freedom to choose, including the freedom to choose to hurt his neighbor, there was nothing God could do to prevent it.

God leaves us to be human, and that includes both our virtues and our vices. There is little doubt that we have an equal capacity to harm people as we do to help them. The crucial issue is learning to sense when our lives are consciously or unconsciously caught up in harmdoing and, in so sensing, to engage in an act of refusal.

Both Kushner and I have spoken of the capacity we have for doing harm to others. What I want to argue, finally, is that harming others is another way in which we often try to protect ourselves against harm. I am not speaking here of an act of self-defense but of a way in which we avoid facing up to our own empty lives and personal degradation.

It might be thought that harming others to protect one's self from harm is obviously self-defeating, but sadly it is all too natural and common for us to do so—and not simply out of retribution. Why then would we choose to do harm? Why do we hurt others? Simone Weil (1909–1943) suggests that because we do not wish to face up to our own degraded character, at the first inkling of our own weakness, our own human wretchedness, we attempt to turn that weakness upon others. Piercing to the heart of the matter, she writes in *Gravity and Grace* (p. 65), "A hurtful act is the transference to others of the degradation which we bear in ourselves. That is why we are inclined to commit such acts as a way of deliverance." What is the force of this remark?

Knowing we have the capacity for evil and harmdoing within us, we seek to deliver ourselves from it; we seek to cast out our pettiness, our greed, and our anger; we seek to rid ourselves of this evil—but in doing this we wrongly direct it toward others and it inflicts harm. Such hurtful acts do, indeed, reflect our own degradation. So Weil says that a hurtful act is the transference of evil from ourselves to others. She urges that we learn to rechannel the evil, our own degradation, into self-affliction and suffering. The point here, of course, is not that we should become masochists but that, by bearing the brunt of our own harmdoing, we seek to purify ourselves. Knowing such evil and feeling its pain, says Weil, "compels the virtue of charity."

Our capacity to hurt others is great, and each hurtful act is a reflection of our own degradation. It is not the subject of the hurtful act who is degraded by it, but the harm-doer. When our self-degradation is accompanied by forms of worldly power, then the potential for hurting increases exponentially with the degree of power we possess. A snipe at a friend, a put-down of a child, a disrespectful act toward a parent shows our self-degradation in a way only less by degree of power than does the tyranny and oppression exercised in the hands of a malevolent ruler. The oppressed are not degraded by the harm done to them; they are, in fact, those who in Christ's view in his Sermon on the Mount are called "blessed" or "happy." The oppressor is the degraded person.

It is with this same awareness that Kushner and Soelle (among others) see God standing on the side of the oppressed, the Jew under fascism, the Armenians at the hands of the Turks, those who suffer in the gulags of the Soviet Union, Argentina, Chile, Guatemala, et al. It is also why a nuclear holocaust is so heinous and degrading an act for those who possess its power. As Kushner concludes (p. 85), "I would like to think that [God] is the source of my being able to feel sympathy and outrage, and that He and I are on the same side when we stand with the victim against those who would hurt him."

If we reflect on Simone Weil's remark from *Gravity and Grace* (p. 110) that "the recognition of human wretchedness is difficult for whoever is rich and powerful," then we, more than some other people, continually avoid facing all these forms of harmful situations. We are, by and large, to be counted among those "rich and powerful," and that alone makes sensing God's spirit more difficult. Note that our wealth may not make our earthly life more difficult, but it does encourage a life that goes on *without God*, and this should pose a problem for all who claim to live in his name. The difficulty is *recognition* of the wretchedness contained in the harm we can do by not sharing our wealth and resources, by evading our penultimate vulnerabilities. The suggestion here is not that we should dwell on disaster, but rather that we see our evasions as an obstacle to sensing the spirit. In all these forms of protection against harm, we set aside awareness of our vulnerabilities and build up our private reserves in order to be able to go it alone. Our private reserves, however, are exhaustible, just as are the natural reserves of this earth.

There is a paradox here. In all that we have said, what seems all too common is the absence of God. But there is in this absence, in all our forgetting, if we can recognize our wretchedness and our human limits, a possibility that the limitlessness of God can break into our hearts and life. We *can* yield when we are forsaken. If we are never forsaken, the need to yield to something beyond ourselves has little occasion to arise in our consciousness.

CHAPTER FOUR

FORGETTING DEATH
AND
THE TRIUMPH OF SECULARISM

We now come to the most difficult deception. We deceive ourselves about death. This is most difficult because it is the deception most easily assimilated in our lives and culture and thus the one least noticed. It was noted in the last chapter that we must see our penultimate vulnerabilities alongside the vulnerability of death. But this was to note that our pursuits are temporary; that we are ultimately like grass—we wither and die. We looked at how we evade our penultimate vulnerabilities by protecting ourselves against harm and by doing harm, but we did not face up to the fact that we also work very hard protecting ourselves against the ultimate vulnerability, our own death.

Two words might characterize our modern life-style: living longer. We seem particularly obsessed with prolonging our life, pushing the boundary of death farther from us, and pursuing the magical, mythical fountain of youth. It is part of our human vanity about which the preacher of the Old Testament was so lyrically eloquent. The preacher knew that God "put eternity into man's mind" and that that might be our undoing. He also knew that the alternative to our search for immortality was "to be happy and enjoy [our]selves as long as [we] live" (Eccl. 3:11–12). This latter point was given a new meaning, however, by Christ's death and life, and it is this new meaning that Christians in particular seem to have forgotten.

Orthodox theologian Alexander Schmemann, in his book *For the Life of the World*, simply noted, "We live in a death-denying culture," and asks, "Where is Christianity in all this?" He answers this question in a most interesting manner, and I want to follow some important features of his argument.

First of all, Schmemann shows that what we call "secularism" is synonymous with a culture that denies death. Secularism is itself a religion that is essentially "life-affirming"; it is a thoroughly systematic form of self-fulfillment behavior, which we have discussed. "Secularism," says Schmemann (p. 98), "is an 'explanation' of death in terms of life." The secularists reconcile themselves with death by saying that "the only world we know is this world, the only life given to us is this life . . . and it is up to us to make it as meaningful, as rich, as happy as possible. Life ends with death." Secularists understand that death is natural, but also that it is unpleasant, so they do all they can to try and forget it. "The best way to forget about death is to be busy, to be useful, to be dedicated to great and noble things, to build an always better world."

I said in Chapter Two that those who decry our secularism have seen things rightly and that our secular abandonment of God has occurred through our individually and incrementally taking charge of our own destinies. Such sovereignty exercised in our earthly life leaves no room for God. Even so, "God" is named by sovereign individuals, not because God is necessary to the meaning of life but because calling on "God" is often convenient in the activities of our social and political life, or because evoking the name of "Christ" is thought, as Schmemann says (p. 109), to promote "the secular value of help in character building, peace of mind, or assurance of eternal salvation." Furthermore, Schmemann says, "the basic religion [the Christian religion, worldwide] that is being preached and accepted as the only means of overcoming secularism is in reality a surrender to secularism." He makes a very strong argument for the fact that Christianity has sought to accommodate secularism and has therefore lost its true meaning. The present-day Christian religion defends the "life-affirming" values of secularism and adjusts its faith to it.

I remarked in Chapter Three that when we ask what we want for our children, our heirs, in this world we must answer the question in terms of our joint happiness and that this happiness has to do with how we live in the face of death. Let me now pursue this point further. What do we mean as Christians by happiness and by living in the face of death? Secularists and religious persons alike know that death ends our biological life, but a central message of the Christian Gospel is that the death and resurrection of Christ changed the meaning of death and life *in this world*. Secularism, and any religion that accommodates secular values, rejects this change of meaning. It rejects what Schmemann calls "epiphany," and, he says (p. 124), "disconnected from that 'epiphany' all is only darkness, absurdity, and death." We will look further in Chapter Nine at how Christ's death and resurrection changes the meaning of life in this world.

There is one last point to be made following Schmemann's insight, and that is about the concept of *helping*. Schmemann has argued that help is a secular value and is deceptive as a genuine Christian value. Help, for him, signifies a form of therapy; that is, whatever religious outlook will help us most in coping better will be adopted. But, as he rightly points out, there are many therapies and other religions that will be of more help in coping with many things in this world than the religion found in the Gospel—it may lead us where we would rather not go! In *Gravity and Grace* (p. 104), Simone Weil said in an even more radical vein, "Religion insofar as it is a sense of consolation is a hindrance to true faith; and in this sense atheism is a purification."

I have been arguing that we do need to be helped and to help others, but my stress has been on our need to *be helped*, rather than on helping as a form of social action or consoling therapy. We cannot go it alone; the burdens of our earthly life need lifting, and this cannot be done by ourselves. This points us beyond ourselves, to the source of epiphany, and it is this fact that needs to be lifted up in our lives if we are to grow in the spirit.

Happiness, from a Christian view, is to be found in our dying to Christ and the recognition that in his death the world was cast in another light, a light in which we are to take joy. Happiness in the sense of the Christian Gospel is to take *joy* in this world, to attend to it, care for it, refuse to yield to its many shifting moods, and love it. Schmemann lifts up this joy in some marvelous passages at the end of his book (pp. 112–113):

> *Honesty* to the Gospel, to the whole Christian tradition, to the experience of every saint and every word of Christian liturgy demands [that we] live in the world seeing *everything* in it as a revelation of God, a sign of His presence, the joy of His coming, the call to communion with Him, the hope for fulfillment in Him. Since the day of Pentecost there is a seal, a ray, a sign of the Holy Spirit on everything for those who believe in Christ and know that He is the life of the world—and that in Him the world in its totality has become again a *liturgy*, a *communion*, an *ascension*. . . . It is only when in the darkness of *this world* we discern that Christ has *already* "filled all things with Himself" that these *things*, whatever they may be, are revealed and given to us full of meaning and beauty. A Christian is the one who, wherever he looks, finds Christ and rejoices in Him. And this joy *transforms* all his human plans and programs, decisions and actions, making all his mission the sacrament of the world's return to Him who is the life of the world.

We must, therefore, not fear our death but see it in the light of the death and the new life of Christ. It is a fundamental claim of the Christian Gospel that Emmanuel, God with us, can change our life, and that our all-consuming struggle to live longer and to protect ourselves is to forget this fact—it is to forget the meaning of the cross and his forgiveness, of the empty tomb and his grace. But the hard thing in our forgetting is *not* deceiving ourselves about the ways in which we say we remember.

With our interests and importance, our protective instincts and our desires, our knowledge and technologies, we find it hard to see this world differently; we find it hard to see beauty in all the suffering, and we find little joy in trying to transform our plans and programs in ways that go against the streams of our daily life. Our energies are used in holding on, not letting go; in taking, not refusing; in fulfilling, not sacrificing. How can we be led in all this death denial—our own death and the death of Christ—toward glimpsing the light and a new life? In the resurrection of Christ, death has been overcome, and to deny death is to deny his victory. Thus, we must live joyfully in the face of *one* death that remains certain because we are transformed through *another* death that broke its sting.

CHAPTER FIVE

THE PARADOX
IN OUR FORGETTING

A family member in a community of Vietnamese refugees struggling to make their way in our alien land recently remarked to a young American woman assisting them, "We live under so many pressures not to love." What an extraordinary and simple indictment of our culture! In our quest for power we have deceived ourselves even about our basic need to love one another. We have come to accept all those pressures "not to love," and in doing so we have become nearly impotent. All our life-affirming and death-denying energies are not giving us the peace we seek. In pursuing what seems good to us, we are exhausting our natural environment, our psychic and moral energies are worn out, and our economic and political policies toward one another in the community of nations are bankrupt.

Furthermore, what we have yet to see clearly, as we make a last frantic gasp after an "ultimate" power we call military power, is that *it will not save us* or bring us peace. We are hostage to an unprecedented world arms race and to our own harnessing of nuclear energy. Six nations, perhaps as many as ten, stand holding in their hands a useless weapon, good only for their own destruction. War, once a final, violent, and decisive strategy used by nations to bridle tyranny, has itself become impotent in the nuclear age. Jonathan Schell, in his book *The Fate of the Earth*, put it bluntly (p. 193): "There is thus no need to 'abolish war' among the nuclear powers; it is already gone. The choices don't include war any longer. They consist now of peace, on the one hand, and annihilation, on the other." Since annihilation is as far from being war as peace is, argues Schell, we have only one real option, some alternative that will save us from self-extermination.

We have gotten ourselves into this nuclear predicament by extension of our deep human need for protection against harm, but ironically the means of protection we have developed only ensures total human destruction, should it be used. Furthermore, we fail, personally and passionately, to face up to this predicament. We deal with it only as an intellectual abstraction or board game. Our denial is a form of self-protection. Schell correctly notes that "anyone who invites people to draw aside the veil and look at the peril face to face is at risk of trespassing on inhibitions that are a part of our humanity" (p. 8).

It should be obvious to us, however, that the first step in turning a peril aside is to look at it face to face, even if that causes us some anxiety or pain. "Trespassing on inhibitions" on such a catastrophic issue as a nuclear holocaust may enable us to see the concept of life in this world differently, just as recognition of Christ's death casts a new light on the meaning of life. The spiritual point in facing up to nuclear peril is that we face up to our ultimate vulnerability in a new way. If, however, we resign ourselves to this peril we are deceiving ourselves again about our own power and moving farther away from accepting God's power over life and death. We are, in fact, making ourselves the god.

Our world is one that borders on forgetting God altogether. For all practical purposes, God has become absent in our earthly life. Our lives are bereft of true devotion and service to God and thus of marshaling any sense of the presence of God in everyday affairs. It is not a nihilistic state I describe, however, because we have given names to those things that provide some meaning, secularized meaning, to our lives: wealth and our human power games, all kinds of psychotherapies, scores of variations on the human potential and self-fulfillment themes, and, not least, hundreds of eligions spanning the globe led by imported gurus and mass-media hucksters. All claim a quick fix or success or salvation—many, even in the name of God.

What all this forgetting and this continued desiring may bode is a new prospect for restoring God's presence, not noticeable under less terrible conditions—*a new prospect of seeing ourselves as prodigals.* Having spent our inheritance, if we can come to some awareness and face our squandered lives, we could become a world of prodigals, a people who, after our strength has failed and while we yet go on desiring, *may have positioned ourselves to remember God.* "It is to the prodigals," as Simone Weil said, "that the memory of their Father's house comes back." Such is our paradox!

If we have positioned ourselves to remember God, why then don't things get better? The truth is that even if such a positioning has occurred, we may not yet be aware of it. We must first *recognize* the predicament we are in, *withhold* ourselves from our self-deceptive behavior, and *engage* in acts of refusal and renunciation: that is, develop a capacity for a new form of self-sacrificial behavior. This is a kind of warfare different from the kinds we are familiar with; it is what Francis de Sales (1567–1622) called in 1609 "spiritual warfare." In his *Introduction to the Devout Life* (p. 41), he wrote:

> The work of purging the soul neither can nor should end except with our life itself. We must not be disturbed at our imperfections, since for us perfection consists in fighting against them. How can we fight against them unless we see them, or overcome them unless we face them? Our victory does not consist in being unconscious of them but in not consenting to them, and not to consent to them is to be displeased with them. To practice humility it is absolutely necessary for us at times to suffer wounds in this spiritual warfare, but we are never vanquished unless we lose our life or our courage.

We could look at all the ways in which we forget God and exclude him from our life as human imperfections. And we could look at the spiritual life as a continual fight against these imperfections. All the ways we have examined by which we forget God—when our words fill all the silent spaces, when self-importance takes up too much room in our life, when we feel lost or impotent, when tragedies darken our lives, when we engage in hurtful acts against others, even our loved ones, when we deny death—should signal God's absence and remind us that our lives are incomplete, limited, and powerless. All are forms of denial, and a life in the spirit is blocked by denial, by the conscious avoidance of living out the gospel and a failure to see in God's Word what we are clearly enjoined to do.

To be aware of these imperfections, *not to consent* to them, *to be displeased* by them, *to have courage* to suffer the wounds of this earthly life *is to restore the possibility of God's presence in the midst of his absence.* In this paradox of God's presence in absence is the core of the spiritual life. The classic theological expression of this paradox is found in John of the Cross's *Dark Night of the Soul.* John of the Cross (1542–1591) says that the purging of our desires, of our pride, of our degrading acts lead toward a "dark night" where great suffering and affliction are felt as one abandons all that was common to the earthly life. As he says, one feels "the deepest poverty and wretchedness . . . and abandonment of the spirit in darkness" (p. 106). And furthermore, "This darkness should continue for as long as is needful in order to expel and annihilate the habit which the soul has long since formed in its manner of understanding, and the Divine light and illumination will then take its place" (p. 121). All this is for the purpose of restoring a sense of the presence of God. Finally, John says (pp. 119f.), in a spirit similar to Schmemann's,

> although this happy night brings darkness to the spirit, it does so only to give it light in everything; and that, although it humbles it and makes it miserable, it does so only to exalt it and to raise it up; and, although it impoverishes it and empties it of all natural affection and attachment, it does so only that it may enable it to stretch forward, divinely, and thus to have fruition and

experience of all things, both above and below, yet to preserve its unrestricted liberty of spirit in them all.

We have tried to expose this paradox on an ordinary plane of our life and not on the theological plane characteristic of so much of the classic spiritual literature. It is when we can look at our forgetfulness, our deceptions, our diversions and denials that the full force of Simone Weil's remark comes home to us: "I should look upon every sin I have committed as a favor of God." It is from this awareness of the paradox that we now turn to discover ways in which we can *remember* God and activate our hearts and lives in his spirit; that we can "stretch forward" and find Christ and rejoice in him, transforming our human plans and programs into a sacrament of new life.

PART II

WAYS OF REMEMBERING GOD

Draw near to God and he will draw near to you. Cleanse your hands, you sinners, and purify your hearts, you men of double mind.

James 4:8

The spirit must . . . have an intimate sense and feeling that it is making a pilgrimage and being a stranger to all things. . . . For this night is gradually drawing the spirit away from its ordinary and common experience of things and bringing it nearer the Divine sense, which is a stranger and an alien to all human ways.

John of the Cross
Dark Night of the Soul

The Christian life is but a constant re-beginning, a return to grace every day, sometimes even every hour, through Him who, after each failure, pardons so that all things should be made new.

Robert Schutz
This Day Belongs to God

CHAPTER SIX

REMEMBERING OURSELVES AND DRAWING NEAR TO GOD

> In Remembrance resides the secret
> of redemption.
>
> The Baal Shem-Tov

Let us recall what Flannery O'Connor said of herself: "I do not lead a holy life . . . my virtues are as timid as my vices." She even confessed to having no "interesting or pleasurable sins"; hers were "the garden variety, pride, gluttony, envy and sloth." Perhaps you are thinking that O'Connor is more like I am, or that it's too bad she cannot recall to mind more "pleasurable sins" now and then! Whatever our thoughts, our own sins do come to mind. Wittgenstein (pp. 28f.) remarked that "consciousness of sin is a real event [that] actually takes place in human life. . . . Those who speak of such things (Bunyan, for instance) are simply describing what has happened to them, whatever gloss anyone may want to put on it." Whether we like the word "sin" or not, you and I know what kind of thing it is and that it is a part of our life. What we are often not aware of is that—again as O'Connor noted—"sin occasionally brings one closer to God," or even more strongly stated by Simone Weil, our sins can be "a favor of God."

In discussing the many ways in which we forget God, we have come progressively from some minor forgettings, like forgetting to read the Bible or hug your child, to the many ways we think about our self-importance. We moved from life's minor wounds and our hurtful acts toward others to those colossal acts of evil of past holocausts and threats of future ones. Through all this, it may have occurred to you to ask, "How do I, with my 'garden variety sins,' fit into such an awesome, all-embracing (and sometimes depressing) picture? Why do you burden me with such a litany of human imperfections? I am not, myself, so 'grandly' imperfect. Forgetting to hug my child will hardly result in such a grossly harmful and wretched life!" Or through it all you may have remembered the last line of the epigraph to Part I by Simone Weil about the prodigal son: "If the son had lived economically he would never have thought of returning." With this in mind, you may have said to yourself, "I am not a prodigal son or daughter, and I am justly miffed by such squandered lives. Whatever someone else may have done, that is their business and not mine. I have prudently planned and saved for the future."

Unfortunately, the futures we each may plan, even the modest ones, are not neatly under our control—"the best-laid plans of mice and men," you know. But more than that, our plans are not ours to execute alone. What about those fellow feelings that well up in us when least expected—when grief strikes us, or we are touched by a kindness, or take joy in our children's achievements? What, even, of those moments of sympathy and compassion, or anger and frustration, that Rabbi Kushner noted? We are left to be human, and human we are. Even if our garden is not a romantic or exotic one, weeds grow near the zinnias and daffodils just the same if it is not constantly tended. However ordinary we may think ourselves to be, each of us is given similar human equipment and must find a way to put it to use in our lives.

Because we are human we have not really forgotten the weeds and the sin; we have only put them out of mind and ceased to notice them. One thing that is certain in our being human is that, by the same token with which we sin, we can also do good; the fact that we can harm others is also a sign that we can help them as well. On the other side of our ceasing to notice is our coming to notice; what becomes absent to our mind can also become present to it. Just as we forget many things, we remember much as well. To remember that we have "an unlimited capacity for doing harm," as Socrates said to his friend Crito, is also to remind ourselves that we "might have an unlimited power for doing good."

Henri Nouwen in *The Living Reminder* brings the notions of forgetting and remembering into helpful focus. He says (p. 17) that "to forget our sins may be an even greater sin than to commit them. Why? Because what is forgotten cannot be healed and that which cannot be healed easily becomes the cause of greater evil." The prodigals, because they see the pits to which they are driven, remember their Father's house. Again we are reminded of the paradox and of the importance of fighting against our forgetfulness. Nouwen again (p. 18) says, "An Auschwitz that is forgotten causes a Hiroshima, and a forgotten Hiroshima can cause the destruction of our world. By cutting off our past we paralyze our future." To put it closer to home, we could say: To forget to nurture our sick children to health can cause an even greater illness, and to forget their emotional needs will lead them to anxiety and distrust of their parents. When our attention turns away from those in need, they are driven to seek help elsewhere and turn away from us. When ordinary people seek only their own self-fulfillment, the bonds of an intradependent human family begin to fall apart. Remember these things. *Healing* is an object of our remembering.

Our memory controls our remembering. Nouwen's *The Living Reminder* is aimed at ministers and their need to become reminders of Christ, serving others and reminding them of the connections between Jesus Christ and ourselves, that our "human wounds are most intimately connected with the suffering of God himself." He is instructing pastors on the awesome responsibility of reminding people of the connections between "our little life and the great life of God with us" (p. 25). In that helpful book, more is said about our memories and remembering than I will review here. But there is one point about remembering ourselves and telling our stories that I want to emphasize. Nouwen writes (p. 19):

The older we grow the more we have to remember, and at some point we realize that most, if not all, of what we have is memory. Our memory plays a central role in our sense of being. Our pains and joys, our feelings of grief and satisfaction, are not simply dependent on the events of our lives, but also, and even more so, on the ways we remember these events. The events of our lives are probably less important than the form they take in the totality of our story. Different people remember a similar illness, accident, success, or surprise in very different ways, and much of their sense of self derives less from what happened than from how they remember what happened, how they have placed the past events into their own personal history.

It is not surprising, therefore, that most of our human emotions are closely related to our memory. Remorse is a biting memory, guilt is an accusing memory, gratitude is a joyful memory, and all such emotions are deeply influenced by the way we have integrated past events into our way of being in the world. In fact, we perceive our world with our memories. Our memories help us to see and understand new impressions and give them a place in our richly varied life experiences.

With this we can see the importance our memories play. We select the good from the bad and retell our stories, leaving much untold. To be a whole person in our complex and troubled time means that more of our earthly story needs to be told, more of its shadings need to be highlighted, and more of our human emotions need revealing so that we can see when help is needed and recognize our mutual dependence.

One chapter of our earthly story that has recently been brilliantly retold is found in the novel *A Model Childhood*, by an East German, Christa Wolf. Here forgetting is confronted by a painful remembering; emotions are revealed and wounds healed. It has been noted how fascism owes its livelihood to forgetting. But the wounds from Hitler's fascism of the 1930s are no more deeply felt than in the generation of

Germans who cannot overcome their own forgetting, a generation now in their fifties and sixties. Christa Wolf begins her novel with these words: "What is past is not dead; it is not even past. We cut ourselves off from it; we pretend to be strangers." The struggle of overcoming oneself enough to find out the truth is at the heart of *A Model Childhood*.

Nelly Jordan's childhood and teen years were from 1933 to 1946. She is caught up in the enthusiasm of a promised greatness for the German race, and she is loyal and unquestioning though often silent when troubled by events that jar the ordinary conscience of a child. It is not difficult to see why one gets caught up. Wolf writes of Nelly's father, a grocer: "When Bruno Jordan had to choose between a vague discomfort in his stomach and the multi-thousand-voice roar coming over the radio, he opted, as a social being, for the thousand and against himself" (p. 43). Wolf is trying to recover herself and come to terms with Nelly's silences and to understand Bruno's "vague discomfort."

In the end, Nelly and the first-person author's narrative voice become one—Nelly becomes "I." She says near the end of the novel, when Nelly has been befriended by a teacher who resisted Hitler in small but clear ways, that one's mind can be sent "on a vacation," that one's conscience can be turned around, against itself. Our memory can serve to show us how we can easily be turned around and what may be required to regain our original conscience. But, as Wolf warns, "Perhaps [we] have as little desire as anyone else to cross borders behind which all innocence stops."

The novel is set in the 1970s, when the author decides to return to her hometown on the Polish frontier to see if she can gather material for a book and reconstruct events of her childhood. She takes with her her teenage daughter, Lenka, who represents a new generation with no firsthand memory of prewar events. The following passage says much about the two different generations and how what is forgotten and what is remembered can separate us so completely.

The author reports about an event in May 1945, when Nelly's family was in flight—themselves now refugees—and found themselves seated with a recently liberated inmate from a concentration camp whose only crime had been the admission of being a Communist. Nelly's mother, Charlotte Jordan, offers him some pea soup and says (p. 39):

> Communist? But just because you were a communist they didn't put you in a concentration camp! And his reply: Where on earth have you all been living. . . . One and a half years later Bruno Jordan returns from Soviet captivity, changed beyond recognition; with shaved head, he sits at the table of strangers [his family], ravenously slurping up the proffered soup. What have they done to us, he says, shaking his head.
>
> (Lenka says: She can't understand it. Sentences like that. Said by people who were there the whole time. She does not wish—not yet—to hear how one could be there and not be there at the same time, the ghastly secret of human beings in this century. She still equates explanation with excuse, and rejects it. She says: One must be consistent. She means: uncompromising. You are very familiar with this need and ask yourself when your uncompromising severity began to disintegrate. A process later known as "maturity.")

The question Lenka prompts is crucial and must be asked of ourselves: When did our uncompromising severity begin to disintegrate? When did we begin to become strangers from ourselves and make a truce with those "vague discomforts" in our stomachs? If our memory stays active, we may spare ourselves yet another explanation for a "ghastly secret." If we learn to remember, we can hope for a future and make room for God to figure in it.

We need to remember ourselves—that we are forgetful, that we have spent too much of our energy consuming, planning, and building, that we hurt others; we need to remember our vague discomforts and sins, great and small alike. To remember ourselves prepares us to remember God. But the route from remembering ourselves to remembering God is not a direct or easy one; it requires a great effort of the spirit, which will lead us where we would rather not go, as the apostle John reminded us, and will take us through many "dark nights," as John of the Cross suggested (he also called such nights "happy" ones!). John of the Cross also noted that such "dark nights" enable the spirit to "stretch forward, divinely." These efforts of the spirit, our stretching forward, involve the active use of our memories at the very least, and such recognitions make us aware of our limitations and our need for help—help from others and from God.

The apostle James said, "Draw near to God and he will draw near to you." In addition to remembering ourselves, we must remember others: our families, our neighbors near and far, our enemies—all are included in God's address to us. As we remember ourselves and others, we learn to draw near to God.

In the tradition of spiritual literature, a central image used to describe efforts made in drawing near to God is the pilgrimage. In addition to the obvious, like Bunyan's allegorical *The Pilgrim's Progress* and *The Way of the Pilgrim* from the Eastern Orthodox tradition, the historical pilgrimage has recently been given a new focus by Victor and Edith Turner in their *Image and Pilgrimage in Christian Culture*. The Turners look at the pilgrimage as a structural and cultural process by which ordinary laypeople have sought to draw near to God. They say that a pilgrimage where one travels to a holy shrine is a form of "exteriorized mysticism . . . the point of it all is to get out, go forth, to a far holy place approved by all" (p. 7). This is in contrast to "an interior pilgrimage" associated with monasticism and the contemplative life.

There is a sense, however, in which a pilgrimage can move us both out and beyond the local constraints of a place and also within, to a confidence of spirit that is a stranger to the prevailing moods of the earthly life. John of the Cross said (p. 123) that "the spirit must have an intimate sense and feeling that it is making a pilgrimage." And although he may have had more of the contemplative model in mind, "making a pilgrimage" can be a way of living in the spirit that involves neither "mysticism" nor travel "to a far holy place."

It can help us cultivate an intimate sense of God's presence to us.

In the following three chapters I suggest a pilgrimage route. Drawing from a variety of sources in both classical and contemporary literature and from God's Word to us, I identify three disciplines of the human spirit, disciplines that we can take up in our day-to-day lives to give us an intimate sense of pilgrimage, a sense of drawing near to God so that God may draw near to us. These disciplines of the human spirit are: (1) *attention* to our earthly life, (2) *refusal and renunciation* of the moods of the world, and (3) *loving God*.

The manner in which we make our pilgrimage and draw near to God affects how we sense God drawing near to us; the exercise of these disciplines of the human spirit prepares us for an active spiritual presence—a presence that shows in our life, the life of Emmanuel, God with us. In the end, if we have come to terms with the ways of forgetting God, then remembering God will appear to us as a return to the obvious.

CHAPTER SEVEN

DISCIPLINE ONE: ATTENTION TO OUR EARTHLY LIFE

A quarter of an hour of attention is better than
a great many good works.

Simone Weil
Waiting for God

The Community of the Ark in France has set for itself a single task: "To make ready a people prepared for the Lord." Making oneself ready and a people ready for the Lord is difficult in view of our forgetfulness. But, as we have seen, awareness of our forgetfulness paradoxically postures us to remember God. For the founder of the Ark, Lanza del Vasto, to make ready for the Lord requires "conversion." He is not specifically talking about the Christian doctrine here (though it is not incompatible) but about paying attention to oneself in order to lose or give oneself: "Self-possession must precede self-giving, for one cannot give what one does not have" (*Make Straight the Way of the Lord*, p. 8). This self-possession for self-giving requires a "spiritual effort," vigilance and struggle with our forgetting and our remembering—it requires that we attend to ourself.

In a similar vein, Thomas Merton (1915–1968) while Novice Master at the Trappist monastery of Gethsemani in Kentucky, instructed the novitiate on the difficulties of the new path they had chosen. Far from leaving the human world behind for some esoteric journey, Merton said to them, "The first step in the love of God is being human. My first obligation to God is to be me." He went on:

> If I love God without first being me, I am cheating Him. I am selling Him a phony bill of goods. If I love God I have got to love Him with my heart. If I love Him with my heart, I have got to have a heart, and I have got to have it in my possession to give. One of the most difficult things in life today is to gain possession of one's heart in order to be able to give it. We don't have a heart to give. We have been deprived of these things, and the first step in the spiritual life is to get back what we have to give and to be ourselves.*(Life and Solitude)*

Throughout this chapter, I want to talk about ways in which we can "get back" our heart in order to give it. A first step is to learn to pay attention, to cultivate a greater capacity for attention. Attention is an extension of remembering ourselves, but it also moves us both out of and beyond this earthly life, to its temporary and changing moods, to its people and their projects, to nature in its ravaging force and pacific grandeur, and to our relation with God.

Attention could be thought of as a discipline of the human spirit that is a step on our pilgrimage route, a step in getting back ourselves and drawing near to God. It combines with recognition and awareness of our forgetting to keep us on a path of greater remembrance; it aids us in keeping our "dark, happy nights" from becoming nights of despair.

A pilgrim is an initiate, a novice—one venturing on a new path. Every pilgrim is faced with the same sins and is confronted by all those things that led to our forgetting and denial. But by deliberately setting out on this journey, the sins and the world can be viewed from a new vantage point. This journey is not for the calculating intellect but is a journey that must be carried out with heartwork. A pilgrim has to face this earthly life with a new resolve, a movement of the heart that is and will remain secret and hidden from the world, rather than with words and virtuosity. Attention is our greatest companion to inner resolve and heartwork. Simone Weil has called such resolve "real desire," where one's heart and mind are focused toward a single final end, the love of God. In *Waiting for God* (pp. 107, 109) she says that "there is a real desire where there is an effort of attention" and that "desire alone draws God down." In her poem "The Threshold," collected in *The Simone Weil Reader* (p. 408), she says:

> We want to see flowers. Here thirst grips us.
> Waiting and suffering, we are here before the door.

One object of the pilgrim is to seek release from the external structures that normally bind us—even the structures of religion itself. But before release is possible, the structures that are binding must be given careful attention. The Turners in their analysis of pilgrimage (p. 15) note the following:

> A pilgrim is one who divests himself of the mundane concomitants of religion—which become entangled with its practice in the local situation—to confront, in a special "far" milieu, the basic elements and structures of his faith in their unshielded, virgin radiance. It is true that the pilgrim returns to his former mundane existence, but it is commonly believed that he has made a spiritual step forward.

Pilgrims, with a proper degree of attention and thus "real desire," can begin to disentangle themselves from practices that have either lost meaning altogether from habitual overuse or impious use or whose meanings have become assimilated to the secular values of our culture, and thus, in turn, to confront their faith in its virgin radiance.

Thomas Merton, again speaking to his novitiate class, said, "Am I a drone? This is a spiritual question." Attention keeps us from being drones. We can think of many ordinary kinds of attention that make life interesting, that keep us from being drones. Let us look at a few.

First there are some sensory experiences that cannot be grasped in a fleeting moment; they require that we attend to them with patience and an open sense of respect. Some, such as the mystery of many forms of biological life seen under a microscopic eye, even take time to unfold before us. Growth, change, division, reproduction: all fascinate, as do the changing hues of a sunset or the sounds and sights of a natural scenic wonder. A solitary child walking in a wood can turn over a rotting stump and attend at length a newly found and busy micro-social order of insects. The ornithologist cannot be hurried in the marsh, nor the chemist in the lab. The master cabinetmaker attends with meticulous tactile care to wood grains and finishes, joints and fittings. All these examples and more provide us with lessons in attention where some object is cared for and respected for its own autonomous qualities. We can think of attention to such objects as requiring a certain time and space, as requiring us to be somewhere without distraction—perhaps even in silence. The value of these sensible experiences, says Simone Weil in *Gravity and Grace* (p. 110), "lies in the greater possibility of attention." Not to take away from their own intrinsic value, we can use such experiences as preliminary to a higher attention. If, for example, we can make a great effort of attention "in the presence of mere matter (. . . the sky, the stars, the moon, trees in blossom)," she asks, what might happen "if we could be attentive to the same degree in the presence of a human being"?

Another area discussed by Simone Weil where our ordinary attentiveness can be seen to point to a higher value is in school studies, a point seldom noticed by students! In an unusual juxtaposition she relates school studies with prayer and says that "each school exercise should be a refraction of spiritual life. There must be method in it. A certain way of doing a Latin prose, a certain way of tackling a problem in geometry (and not just any way) make up a system of gymnastics of the attention calculated to give it a greater aptitude for prayer" (ibid., pp. 108f.).

It may seem a giant leap to go from geometry to prayer, but let me develop her point a bit further from her most interesting essay, entitled "Reflections on the Right Use of School Studies with a View to the Love of God." In this essay, collected in *Waiting for God*, she argues that school ex-

ercises develop "a lower kind of attention," but the pearl in
this for adolescents is that such exercises *can* be "extremely
effective in increasing the power of attention that will be
available at the time of prayer," provided the studies are approached with the "higher" purpose in mind and not carried out for grades or under threat of reprisal. Students
should apply themselves equally to all tasks and not show
preference to one subject over another, for the importance
here is "increasing the power of attention" rather than win-
ning school success. An unnoticed feature in this process is
giving close attention to "each school task in which we have
failed . . . trying to get down to the origin of each fault"
without complaint or excuse. She notes that the temptation
is great to overlook the faults. But if the purpose is to prepare ourselves for the love of God, we must not refuse to
give attention to our faults. Attention to faults helps in ac-
quiring the virtue of humility.

She defines attention in this way (pp. 111f.): "Attention
consists of suspending our thought, leaving it detached,
empty, and ready to be penetrated by the object. . . . Above
all, our thought should be empty, waiting, not seeking anything, but ready to receive in its naked truth the object that
is to penetrate it." Not to give this kind of attention to school
studies has its consequences: "All wrong translations, all ab-
surdities in geometry problems, all clumsiness of style, and
all faulty connection of ideas in compositions and essays . . .
are due to the fact that thought has seized upon some idea
too hastily, and being thus prematurely blocked, is not open
to the truth" (p. 112).

At the conclusion of this essay, Weil moves us back and
forth between school studies and the importance of attention for the love of God and the love of our neighbor. The
following paragraphs (pp. 114f.) speak directly to why this
kind of attention is so important to our pilgrimage.

> Not only does the love of God have attention for its
> substance; the love of our neighbor, which we know to
> be the same love, is made of this same substance. Those
> who are unhappy have no need for anything in this

world but people capable of giving them their attention. The capacity to give one's attention to a sufferer is a very rare and difficult thing; it is almost a miracle; it *is* a miracle. Nearly all those who think they have this capacity do not possess it. Warmth of heart, impulsiveness, pity are not enough.

In the first legend of the Grail, it is said that the Grail belongs to the first comer who asks the guardian of the vessel, a king three-quarters paralyzed by the most painful wound, "What are you going through?"

The love of our neighbor in all its fullness simply means being able to say to him: "What are you going through?" It is a recognition that the sufferer exists, not only as a unit in a collection, or a specimen from the social category labeled "unfortunate," but as a man, exactly like us, who was one day stamped with a special mark by affliction. For this reason it is enough, but it is indispensable, to know how to look at him in a certain way.

This way of looking is first of all attentive. The soul empties itself of all its own contents in order to receive into itself the being it is looking at, just as he is, in all his truth.

Only he who is capable of attention can do this.

So it comes about that, paradoxical as it may seem, a Latin prose or a geometry problem, even though they are done wrong, may be a great service one day, provided we devote the right kind of effort to them. Should the occasion arise, they can one day make us better able to give someone in affliction exactly the help required to save him, at the supreme moment of his need.

What Simone Weil says about attention and the love of our neighbor recalls Rabbi Kushner's (and Dorothee Soelle's) comment cited in Chapter Three about standing with the afflicted and being aware of our vulnerability. The act of emptying, here, is to have found one's self in a way adequate to giving one's self; it is to have a heart to give. It is also a sign that God's grace is working through us and that we are not simply acting out of impulse. In this way Simone Weil draws our attention to the role of truth as God's grace, as a given from God to the person who by attention has learned to wait, to care for an object (natural, human, or divine), and to show compassion and love. In fact, the name Simone Weil gives to the right kind of attention in her "Human Personality" is "love" (*Two Moral Essays*, p. 31).

The Bible itself is full of stories that stress our vigilance and attention, all for the sake of waiting for the grace of God to work and to teach us that we cannot take charge. I call your attention to the foolish virgins in Luke and to the lack of vigilance in the disciples at Gethsemane.

Let me review some lessons and note some pitfalls in connection with these examples. First of all, as a discipline of the human spirit, attention must be exercised for the higher purpose of the love of God. It is easy and quite common, for example, to simply stare at something in nature. Usually when we stare at something we do not take notice of it as it is; rather, we fix our eye muscles in its direction. Or we could appear to be giving an object our attention and instead be miles away, daydreaming. Here we would be seeking something completely different from the object of immediate attention.

It may also become quite routinized to do the geometry problems and thus be simply an exercise in mental gymnastics. Often we say to ourselves, "Now concentrate!" and we tense our muscles and furrow our brow. But this, as Simone Weil noted, is simply a kind of "muscular effort" and "ends by making us tired." Another way of looking at this would be to note that heartwork is missing when only the mind and muscles are being worked. As we say, "Our heart is not in it." In all these cases there is no real attention, and we fail to penetrate the object.

There is another pitfall where, in a sense, attention is involved, but the kind of attention hinders it from serving us as a spiritual discipline. This is to give attention to an object for the purpose of the pleasure we may derive from it. For example, we could give inordinate attention to our automobile for the sake of the enjoyment it brings us. Or a walk in the woods might be simply for an aesthetic high. Neither of these enjoyments that involve our attention is bad, but each has its own end, which probably will not hold value toward the end of remembering God.

Lanza del Vasto has given some very practical advice to help us avoid these pitfalls and others and to aid us in turning attention into a real discipline of the spirit. I will discuss only two of several exercises he prescribes in his *Make Straight the Way of the Lord*. Both are adaptable to our ordinary lives and quite different in nature from taking up some more formal discipline like yoga or aerobics or TM.

In this first exercise he addresses the very real problem of our scattered consciousness and our inability to focus on a single thing for very long. We tend to want to do too many things at once. This, of course, is an outgrowth of the times in which we live. We simply do not seem to know how to stop and look, and we end up expending a lot of muscular effort. Here is an exercise to try (pp. 27f.):

> The first exercise we recommend to you, busy friend, you who have so many important things to do and so little time, will not take you an hour, half an hour, or even a quarter of an hour, but three minutes. . . . And perhaps three minutes is still too much, so let us divide them into six: six times a day, three times in the morning, and three times in the afternoon, be still. Stop!
>
> You are in a hurry? All the more reason for checking yourself. You have things to do? Stop, otherwise you will make mistakes. You have to look after other people? All the more reason for beginning with yourself, lest you harm those others.
>
> So, unharness. Relax. For half a minute every two hours, stop! Put down what you have in your hand. Hold yourself straight. Breathe deeply. Draw your senses inward. Suspend yourself before the inner dark, the inner void. And even if nothing happens, you will have broken the chain of haste. . . . To recollect oneself is to gather up all the shreds of oneself that were

dispersed and clinging to things here and there. Answer as Abraham answered God's call: "Present" (*Adsum!*).

The exercise consists, then, in remaining present to oneself and to God for half a minute. . . .

It is unlikely that in so short a time you will plunge deeply into the mystery of self, but it is not impossible with the grace of God. However, even if nothing else happens during the moment of suspension, we shall at least have broken the chain of events that held us prisoner. We shall have broken it in six and taken the first step toward deliverance.

Lanza del Vasto refers to this as an exercise of "recall"—recalling your self to yourself. He also points out that it serves to help us remember ourselves, both in terms of how we have gotten caught up in our busyness and also how we have a self that needs recalling. This exercise may serve us well as a step toward being attentive—attentive to all the ways we have forgotten God, attentive to ourselves, and to all aspects of our earthly life.

There is another exercise he recommends that we can all also practice. This he calls a "perpetual exercise" as distinct from the three-minute one. He outlines this perpetual exercise as follows (pp. 34f., emphasis added):

This is the name I give to an exercise one can do in any circumstances and which neither suspends nor deviates the habitual course of one's daily actions. It can be done at any time, therefore you can devote all your time to it.

It is the exercise of double attention or redoubled attention.

It consists in concentrating your attention on yourself in action.

Not just paying attention to the object, to the purpose, to your work, but *to yourself seeing the object, yourself going toward the goal, yourself at work.*

Which amounts to relating everything to the inner

center and centering yourself in what you are doing.

It is not enough to pay attention to what you are doing. You must pay attention to yourself doing what you
are doing. . . .

It requires no change in one's occupation or manner,
yet the sense, the density, the value of all one's acts are
wholly changed.

This exercise is a little more difficult to grasp, but let's break
it down and think of some ways it might work. First of all,
your attention is on yourself *in action*. Whatever it is that you
are doing, the focus of attention is on *the way* you are doing
it.

A Benedictine sister of Oulton Abbey in Staffordshire, England, said to me and a small group of students living with
their community, "You can learn more about a person by the
way she handles a broom than by what she says." Am I
aware of how I am handling the broom? Or we could ask, as
we did before, "Is our heart in it?"—in our sweeping, our
running, our calculating, our translating, our caring for the
sick, our cooking? Is our running for pleasure in order to win
or is it, as it was for the Scotsman and Olympian Eric Lid-
dell in *Chariots of Fire*, "for God"? How am I "seeing," looking at, the guardian of the Grail? Am I looking at him with
envy for his nearness to the sacred cup or with compassion
for his great pain? By such attention to ourself in action we
gain a heightened awareness of our strengths and weaknesses, our denials and deceptions, our harmdoing and our
death-denying activities.

The change that this exercise of attention can bring about
is not, as Lanza del Vasto said, in one's occupation or manner but, quite dramatically, in one's way of regarding one's
self as an agent and actor in the world, as one who meets
the public every day and becomes aware of motives and
manners every moment. It is "relating everything to the inner center and centering yourself" in order to have a firm
hold of what it is that you have to give to others and to God.

Finally, prayer is a part of the discipline of attention. One
would expect a whole book to be required at this point, and

a fair expectation that is. I wish, however, only to add briefly to the point that prayer is a part of our higher attention and that all we have said about learning to cultivate the attention in small and ordinary ways can and will serve the end of the love of God in prayer.

Jean Nicolas Grou (1731–1803), known as Père Grou, published his *Spiritual Maxims* in 1789, and like Francis de Sales's *Devout Life,* this book had a particularly strong appeal to beginners in the disciplines of the spirit—it is directed toward those who live an ordinary life and who seek to improve their devotion to God.

In the fifteenth maxim, Père Grou discusses difficulties in prayer. However noble and faithful our prayer life may be, we will suffer long periods of "dryness," where distraction and weariness and loss of hope and anguish over many setbacks in our life will interrupt our attentiveness at all levels. As Père Grou says (p. 171), "Those who suffer [dryness] are very subject to distraction. But these are inevitable, and torture many good souls who fancy them wilful, and cannot get rid of them, no matter what they do." These may appear to be signs of God's absence, but paradoxically, if we continue to desire God through it all, his presence will be made known in ways that "pass our understanding." Père Grou tells us to "suffer dryness with a good heart." If we have learned to be attentive to all aspects of our earthly life, then suffering dryness will not be difficult. We will find it easier to live with the self we possess even though God may appear absent from us.

Père Grou is very much aware of the many distractions that wander into our times of prayer; "without warning, my imagination goes off at a tangent, and is occupied with a thousand different things" (p. 171). When this happens, Grou says, we must work to "remain quietly in the presence of God" and struggle not to "consent" to the diversions. Even more to our point of the relationship between our "lower" and "higher" forms of attention, Père Grou says (p. 172):

Usually we bring to our prayer the same state of mind

in which we are accustomed to live. God will not work a miracle to keep us recollected, and we will in vain endeavour to be so if at other times we suffer our mind and heart to wander as they please.

The habit of attention at every level of our life is crucial to our love of God. If we can Stop!, if we can recall the origins of the distractions and not entertain them as they arise, letting them pass through and out of mind as easily as they entered, and if we can attend to the way we find ourselves praying, then we will be given the grace to remain at peace with ourselves and in the presence of God.

However and wherever we choose to pray, we should do so with all the attentiveness to God we can muster, and it will more than likely be in proportion to the amount of attention we have become accustomed to give to the ordinary aspects of our earthly life—to the natural world, to ourselves, and to our neighbors. As with so many things, attention to God requires practice, and that practice can begin with the stars and the moon, with lacemaking or Latin prose.

Finally, François Fénelon (1651–1715) said this about the practice of prayer:

Do not think that it is necessary to pronounce many words. To pray is to say, Let thy will be done; it is to form a good purpose; it is to raise your heart to God; it is to lament your weakness; it is to sigh at the recollection of your frequent disobedience. (*Selections*, p. 99)

This last phrase, "to sigh at the recollection of [our] frequent disobedience," sums up what I experience so often in prayer. It is, however, at the heart of remembering God. When that sigh comes, if it is deep and contrite, we have released ourself for remorse and confession, and this is a step in drawing near to God.

I said earlier that attention is our greatest companion to inner resolve and heartwork. It places us before the door; it enables us to look in the right way upon this earthly life. When we learn to see the flowers, the sunsets, the microscopic worlds, ourselves in action, *and* a human being in the same way, we have come a long way along our pilgrimage route. We have begun to learn how to take objects, ourselves, and others more seriously. We learn to empty ourselves to find ourselves. We grow in sensitivity and appreciation as well as care and concern. By this we gain a certain confidence of spirit *without* conceit. We feel more confident in a world of lions and lepers; we know how to wait and look rather than turning away or hurriedly passing by on the other side, and we have a new grasp on what it means to possess ourself in order to give ourself. "Suffer dryness with a good [and attentive] heart." With this comes a new way of being present to God in prayer and in life.

When the Countess of Gramont wrote to her spiritual adviser, Fénelon, she often seemed carried away in a self-reveling piety. This Fénelon could not abide, and once he responded: "Come back and be human, Madame, while waiting for charity to rule your heart. [Open your eyes to your own prejudice and] forgive others for being so. . . . Restrain yourself. . . . Eat your pride without being discouraged. Try to calm yourself in silence before God" (*Spiritual Letters of Fénelon*, p. 50). These all require our attention—attention with a view toward the love of God—and it is the love of God that is the goal of the first discipline of the human spirit. But we must remember to be human while we wait for God to draw near to us.

CHAPTER EIGHT

DISCIPLINE TWO: REFUSAL AND RENUNCIATION OF THE MOODS OF THE WORLD

> Religion that is pure and undefiled before God
> and the Father is this: to visit orphans and wid-
> ows in their affliction, and to keep oneself un-
> stained from the world.
>
> James 1:27

This second discipline of the human spirit, which I call refusal and renunciation, is the most difficult for us to undertake. On our pilgrimage we have a sporting chance to cultivate attention, even that higher attention which has its eye
ultimately on the love of God. There are numerous side ben-
efits to our purest acts of attention. Attention to all aspects
of this earthly life results in our being better human beings
and in our world being more humane and tolerable overall.
Of course, a pilgrimage could end with Discipline One and
not be a wasted journey, but it would still be a long distance
from its goal of drawing near to God.

Discipline Two is a *breakaway discipline*. It calls for us to
break away (or at least veer) from the world's path; to follow
God's path and Christ's call to us even if they take us where
we would rather not go. John of the Cross wrote that we
must have an intimate sense of "making a pilgrimage and being a stranger to all things" (p. 123). The intimacy of pilgrimage begins with attention, and one of the results of the right
kind of attention is greater self-possession. Such possession

gives us more confidence in ourselves and is preparation for self-giving. Because self-giving (a form of self-sacrificial behavior) is the antithesis of the natural desire for self-interest and self-fulfillment behavior, it can begin to make us feel like strangers in our own land. We begin to feel "alien to all human ways."

If we have practiced Lanza del Vasto's perpetual exercise and attended to ourselves in action—a whole gambit of actions in daily life—we have most likely seen many things about ourselves that displease us. No doubt we will have run up against our "frequent disobedience," our sin, both our garden-variety sins and our more exotic ones, with a sigh.

As we become aware of such sins and our displeasure with them, we have embarked upon a significant campaign in our "spiritual warfare"—a warfare characterized earlier by Francis de Sales as a fight against our imperfections. As we noted in Chapter Five, Francis de Sales asked, "How can we fight against [our imperfections] unless we see them, or overcome them unless we face them?" And he responded to his question, "Our victory does not consist in being unconscious of them but in not consenting to them, and not to consent to them is to be displeased with them." Displeasure over most sins is contrary to the very nature of the sin: that is, its immediate pleasure to us. So the nature of "spiritual warfare" is somehow wrapped up in our not consenting to what may naturally bring us the greatest pleasure or enhance our self-importance. The warfare of this pilgrimage requires that we engage in *acts of refusal*. It is in this discipline of the spirit that we declare our spiritual independence.

Spiritual independence is quite different from the kind of independence tied up with our Northern, Western values—those values of personal and national sovereign self-reliance. Spiritual independence acknowledges with the author of Wisdom that "God is the guide even of wisdom" and that we, with our words, our understanding, and our skill, "are in his hand."

Putting this in a different and more positive mode, Francis de Sales said that "a strong, resolute soul can live in the world without being infected by any of its moods" (p. 28). If a prevailing mood of our world, as we have seen, is that we take charge of our own affairs, then not being infected by that mood must be a goal of our pilgrimage. Taking charge is contrary to resolutely submitting ourselves to God's wisdom and guidance. We must learn to renounce our own power and let God's power guide us.

A goal of the spiritual life is to free ourselves from circumstances that hinder love and service to God. Such freedom has its price. By engaging in acts of refusal and by renouncing our own power, we make ourselves strangers and may feel "alien to all human ways." Such is the warfare we call spiritual.

This breakaway discipline of refusal and renunciation of the moods of the world requires the greatest of efforts of the spirit; it requires quality acts of attention and a significant degree of self-possession. With these we can practice the art of refusal with both confidence and hope. As we learn the art of refusal, self-renunciation will follow with little difficulty. This will be so because as we face up to and dispossess ourselves of the power characteristic of the moods of the world, God's power can possess us and help us to overcome these moods and replace them with the life of the world found in the cross of Christ.

Let us turn now to some ways in which we can learn this art of refusal. This discipline of the human spirit boils down to the practice of saying no to more, when less will do; to refusing the temptations caught in the net of our self-importance; to accepting help when we might otherwise go it alone; to refusing to harm others and taking our own degradation upon ourselves; to pointing to injustice and oppression when it surfaces in our lives; and to refusing to deny death when exposing its many potential forms may yield life to ourselves and our heirs.

A tool for learning this art of refusal is to train ourselves to see it exemplified in the lives of others who have practiced the art when it seemed most difficult to do so. We can, as William Gass suggested (see Chapter Two), remember "those lovely things and honored people, those vile seduc-

ers and rudy villains," that pass through the changing
moods of our earthly life.

I will turn attention directly to such "honored people"—
the people of Le Chambon-sur-Lignon and their Protestant
pastor, André Trocmé, during the German occupation of
France from 1939 to 1944. The story of this town "and how
goodness happened there" is told by my undergraduate philosophy professor, Philip Hallie, in his moving book *Lest Innocent Blood Be Shed*. To share a small part of this book is to
take a giant step on our pilgrimage. The story of the people
of Le Chambon is one of radical spiritual independence,
where their confidence and hope was drawn from their
watchfulness and their devotion to God. They practiced the
art of refusal and renunciation by their careful attention to
harmdoing and their refusal to do harm. It was from their
resolute love of God that their care for others naturally
flowed.

As Hallie puts it (p. 10), the struggle of the Chambonnais
"flew in the face of . . . self-interest"; it was a struggle
against a "surrounding world of violence, betrayal, and indifference." At the risk of their own destruction they knew,
in the words of their leader, that "it is evil to deliver a
brother who has entrusted himself to us. That we would not
consent to" (p. 104). Not to consent, either to the evil of betrayal or to the violence being done to the Jews required a
great amount of heartwork and much practice in the art of
refusal. The paradox in their story is that by their acts of refusal they became the most human of God's children the
more they became "alien to all human ways."

One of the important lessons to be learned from their story
is that acts of refusal must not all be spontaneous. We must
not put ourselves in all eleventh-hour situations and then
courageously and dramatically respond like a Luther at
Worms with his refusal to recant, nor should we allow ourselves always to be forced into situations that seem to call for
martyrdom. Rather, we should, by our attention to this
earthly life, anticipate the harm that will come if a course is
not changed, the danger that will result from our forgetting.
As Hallie noted about the Chambonnais (pp. 106f., empha-

sis added), they "cared about what *had* happened, and cared enough not only to feel pain at the suffering of the victims but also enough to make inferences about *future* events. They cared enough to think and plan. . . . They cared enough to watch events closely and to see that there was a pattern. . . . [Their] experiences had prepared [them] to care. Living in the spirit requires that we prepare ourselves to care. It requires watchfulness and attention and a life that trains itself for refusal.

This preparation of the Chambonnais led to acts with further consequences for their lives. Because they were prepared to care they actively sought to *prevent* harmdoing and injustice. Hallie comments (p. 110):

> Ordinarily, people have a strong obligation only to avoid doing harm themselves; they are not usually obliged to go out of their way to do anything that will *prevent others* from hating, hurting, or deceiving. It is usually enough if they simply sit quietly within the limits laid down by the "you shall not's" and do nothing to violate those limits.

But because the Chambonnais understood God's Word as command and not just a useful suggestion,

> they must both refuse to do harm themselves and act to prevent others from doing harm, as if they were all being commanded to be the Good Samaritan of Luke 10:30–37, and as if *this* was what Jesus meant when he said, immediately before the Good Samaritan passage, "You shall love the Lord your God with all your heart, and with all your strength, and with all your mind; and your neighbor as yourself."

It was this continual preparedness to care that made refusal so natural for those in the village of Le Chambon. This was expressed with purity and urgency by Madame Eyraud, the wife of a *très chic* member of the Maquis (resistance movement), who, when asked by Hallie (p. 127) "why she found it necessary to let those refugees into her house, dragging after them all those dangers and problems," replied, "Look. Look. Who else would have taken care of them if we didn't? They needed our help, and they needed it *then*." And also by Magda Trocmé, the practical wife of the spiritual leader of the village, André, whose words to her first refugee who appeared at her doorstep were "Naturally, come in, and come in" (p. 120). In these responses was a welcoming attitude that went beyond mere hospitality. It was rooted in an ethic of refusal, and such an ethic is not the ordinary human ethic but an ethic based on the great and second commandments of Christ.

These acts of refusal do not imply that Madame Eyraud or Magda Trocmé or the Chambonnais were revolutionaries. They could not even identify themselves with the violence of the growing resistance movement around them. They were, in short, simply living out the gospel—living in the spirit. For Magda, as she said, "Helping Jews was more important than resisting Vichy and the Nazis" (p. 128).

It must be noted that the *help* given here is not, again, just the humanitarian gesture that anyone might undertake who had sufficient courage and a centered heart. It was help that "came from the Lord." It did so in the sense that the courage and the centeredness for the heartwork that followed "drew its power from the life and death of Jesus Christ." This was André Trocmé's understanding of himself, and it infected his parishioners. He helped at the same time that he strove "to be close to Jesus and, in Jesus, to God. For him, ethical demands had a vertical axis and a horizontal one, like the cross" (p. 162).

Our pilgrimage at certain points may require this breakaway discipline from the ordinary affairs of human life; it may require that we become strangers to this world. When these moments arise, we must be ready to refuse the prevailing moods of the established order: to renounce the world and, with assured self-possession, readily dispossess ourselves. In this way we give ourselves for the sake of a world alive with the light of Christ's spirit.

Our times may be less hard than theirs, and also the sense of urgency that calls up our courage seems far less imminent, but there is an immediately applicable lesson we can learn from the story of Le Chambon—a lesson that has very specific application if we have attended carefully to our nuclear predicament or to injustice and oppression in the name of either "democracy" or "communism." The lesson, again, requires our preparedness and refusal, perhaps even renunciation. It is the lesson that *we must provide hope for our children*. André Trocmé and his Quaker friend Burns Chalmers (whose Society of Friends and the Fellowship of Reconciliation had resources to finance what Le Chambon was to embark upon) shared the same goals of helping those who were victims, but they also had a particular vision (p. 134):

> They wanted to give the children of the refugees a strong feeling and a solid knowledge that there were human beings *outside their own family* who cared for them. Only by *showing* them that human beings could help strangers could they give those children hope and a basis for living moral lives of their own. The most obvious way of doing this was to alleviate the suffering of those children.

With this vision, the primary mission of Le Chambon became that of making the village a place of refuge for children where they would be boarded, nourished, and educated. Chalmers saw Trocmé and his village as a place where good might triumph over evil; where the light of Christ might overcome the darkness of the time. The vision of Le Chambon forces us to ask ourselves, How can we provide our children with a basis for living moral lives on their own? How, as Christians, can we *show* our children a hopeful way of living in the spirit that diminishes suffering in this world and prepares them for acts of refusal? Finally, Hallie concludes about the Chambonnais (p. 284, emphasis added):

> If we would understand the goodness that happened in Le Chambon, we must see *how easy it was* for them to refuse to give up their consciences, to refuse to participate in hatred, betrayal, and murder, and to help the desperate adults and the terrified children who

knocked on their doors. . . . Goodness is the simplest
thing in the world, and the most complex, like opening
a door.

What would it be like to make acts of refusal easy or to be
able to open our door without fear and say "Come in, and
come in?" There are more refugees from violence, oppression, and hunger today than in any time in human history.
The difference is that they do not knock on our doors but appear only as electronic apparitions (not flesh and blood) on
our TV screens or as verbal appendages to a page of global
bad news in our daily newspapers. We have millions of tons
of grain rotting in silos and open fields and millions of dol-
lars being spent on its storage in order *not to* make it available to those in need. Virtually every poor nation in the
world is being destabilized and devastated by a major northern power's unprecedented arms production, sale, and military aid to oppressive governments or to so-called "liberat-
ing" counter movements. While many remain without
bread, few remain without arms. What will it require of us
to overcome our denial of death as embedded in our failure
of response to the nuclear peril? How long can we maintain
what Christa Wolf called the "ghastly secret" that we are
both here and not here at the same time?

Dostoyevsky in *The Brothers Karamazov* reminds us, too, of
the children. "What am I to do about them?" asks Ivan, cit-
ing a litany of horrible stories about children who suffer unjustly. He cries out to Alyosha (pp. 281ff.):

The innocent must not suffer for another's sins, and especially such innocents. . . . I say nothing of the sufferings of grown-up people, they have eaten the apple,
damn them, and the devil take them all! But these little
ones! . . . if the sufferings of children go to swell the
sum of sufferings which was necessary to pay for truth,
then I protest that the truth is not worth such a price.

There is bitterness and resignation in Ivan's lament, but he
will not consent to such suffering or to doctrines that allow
it for the sake of harmony or reason. Here, the rationaliz-

ings are like the process Christa Wolf said we call "maturity," when our "uncompromising severity begins to disintegrate."

When I remember Ivan's remark that "the innocent must not suffer for another's sins" and I think about my own two children, I wonder how it is possible for them to escape the suffering I cannot prevent. There is linkage from past to present to future. But the linkage is not like those chains we see vertically frozen to support a rural mailbox. Just as we create our own past by how we remember it, we can create our future by how we act now in planning for it.

Christa Wolf says in *A Model Childhood*, as she reconstructs Nelly's [her] life late in the war years, when things are going badly for the Germans: "*Verfallen*—a German word. . . . No other language knows *verfallen* in the sense of 'irretrievably lost, because enslaved by one's own, deep-down consent' " (p. 288). If, after we have given attention to every aspect of this earthly life, we then consent to its current moods, we are *verfallen;* we have, theologically, suffered an irretrievable fall from the grace of God—we are lost. If, on the other hand, our attention results in our *not* consenting—even to some of the moods—then we are turned toward God and may draw near to him; "so soon as Faithful talks of heartwork . . . into the wane [we go]." Not to consent and acts of refusal are usually the same.

The Chambonnais learned to make, as Hallie said, "little moves against destructiveness." They watched for signs of harmdoing in others and in themselves; they lifted up the lie and deceit so that no one could fail to see them. Daniel Berrigan, in his poetic *Ten Commandments for the Long Haul*, remarked, "Truth has its own power . . . don't get in the way. . . . But this is not all. The power of Jesus dispels the chimera" (pp. 24, 67). He asks: "What do you do with your life when your life is irretrievably stuck? Answer: Your choices are narrow, but there are still choices. You either (1) stop living, thus adding another corpse to the ethical ossuary, or (2) you get unstuck, you walk out on the death scene, responsibly" (p. 69). With the help of Jesus and the truth, we can get unstuck; we are not "irretrievably lost." *Responsibly* to "walk out on the death scene" is like learning the art of refusal. This is an essential discipline of our spiritual pilgrimage.

Civil disobedience is a recognizable form of refusal. When the Chambonnais took in a Jewish child it was against the law of the state. If we take in a Salvadoran refugee child, it would be against the law of our state! Nelly Jordan's words might reverberate today: "But just because you, Father Berrigan, put paint on a nuclear warhead they didn't put you in prison! And his reply: Where on earth have you all been living?"

A priest and a Levite would not associate with the one beaten and robbed, but the Samaritan (a stranger in the land) did. No one would associate with the beaten, dying Kitty Genovese on a Brooklyn street corner. Lenka, in *A Model Childhood*, asks us (p. 157): "What does a person feel who photographs murders in the course of their assignments, instead of trying to prevent the murders?" What kind of person is "behind the camera . . . instead of helping?" Lenka, who fails to understand the pressures her parents were under, demands "unconditional involvement." Wolf's response to Lenka is to fall silent and remember how easy it was to become a spectator, even to comment on the violence rather than to stop it. There is no such thing as *unconditional* involvement. We know this. But why then the other choice? Why do we so often join the spectators, those Thomas Merton called the "guilty bystanders"?

Preventing others from doing harm can take many forms—civil disobedience as an act of refusal is one, and refusing to be a bystander is another. Still another form of refusal is restraining oneself from doing harm to others. This form of the discipline of refusal and renunciation is equally hard to practice. It too requires training and an effort of the spirit.

Simone Weil refers to such self-restraint as "self-affliction." Let us recall her remark from Chapter Three: "A hurtful act is the transference to others of the degradation which we bear in ourselves." In *Gravity and Grace* she commented on this remark by saying, "When there is a transference of evil, the evil is not diminished but increased in him from whom it proceeds" (p. 65). This she calls the "phenomenon of multiplication." "Where then," she asks, "are we to put the evil?" And she answers (p. 66), "We have to transfer it from the impure part to the pure part of ourselves, thus changing it into pure suffering. The crime which is latent in us we must inflict on ourselves. . . . Patience consists in not transforming suffering into crime." Self-affliction, this suffering turned back upon ourselves, means we give attention to our own self-degradation—our hate and anger, our pride, our greed and gluttony—and turn that degradation "to the good side" in us. This may mean we suffer the "dark, happy night" so that we can submit ourselves to God, now as a specific act of refusal—the refusal to harm others because of our own degradation. This may mean eating our pride, times of less food and material comforts, or biting our tongue to suppress our rage. It will mean that when we might otherwise lash out in hurtful ways to a friend or family member, a policeman or a public servant, we should practice self-restraint: Stop, attend to them, swallow our anger and pride. These, along with being acts of refusal, are also acts of self-purification, and, as Simone Weil also remarked, such acts "compel the virtue of charity." The *virtue of charity* is part of the third discipline of the human spirit to be practiced on our pilgrimage, and to it we will turn shortly.

Postscript. One of the definitions of "discipline" is that of training meant to improve behavior, particularly moral behavior. There is truth to the adage "It's the trying that counts." A discipline of the spirit is a resolute try at Christian behavior.

The discipline of the spirit I call refusal and renunciation begins with "little moves against destructiveness" and ends with loving God. The little moves may be to say again to your child, or your spouse, "I'm sorry," or "I forgive you," or to hug them or give them a kind word that represses your anger or rage. It is that self-affliction that you take upon yourself to avoid hurting others. It is awareness of your own wretchedness and a denial that you can rid yourself of it by your own power. A discipline of the spirit is resolute attention that may demand resolute refusal to lie, to deceive, to obey, to hurt, to deny death. It is a resolve to possess one's self in a way that makes it easy to give one's self, to open the door and say "Come in, and come in." Such a discipline is not possible unless we declare our spiritual independence and train ourselves to draw near to God so that God may draw near to us.

CHAPTER NINE

DISCIPLINE THREE: LOVING GOD

Only he who has measured the dominion of force, and knows how to respect it, is capable of love and justice.

Simone Weil
The Iliad or the Poem of Force

The first part of this book could be summarized in these words of François Fénelon: "We undertake to do everything *without God;* therefore we do not succeed. . . . Without him, all our designs, however good they may appear to be, are only temerity and delusion." If for no other reason than our lack of success, we should take notice of our lives and want to learn how to be *with God.* Fénelon exhorts us: "It is with God, that we must lay our plan of virtue and usefulness" (*Selections,* p. 101). What is the key to laying such a virtuous and useful plan with God? The key is practicing the three disciplines of the human spirit: to attend to our earthly life, to refuse and renounce the moods of the world, and to love God.

But what of this third discipline? Nothing takes greater resolve than loving God—it calls for the greatest effort of the spirit, because we are so inclined to forget him. This effort of the spirit involves breaking away from having our life determined by worldly concerns. It involves measuring "the dominion of force," learning to respect it and sometimes to renounce it. And it means we must depend more upor

God's help as we live in and through a loving and just relationship with our neighbors.

There is no more dramatic rendering of the importance of sensing God's spirit than in the great and second commandments of Christ. These brief and direct commands to love God with all our heart, our mind, and our soul, and to love our neighbors as ourself go hand in hand. Perhaps the clearest and most challenging texts in Scripture that unfold the meaning of these commandments are the twenty-fifth chapter of the Gospel of Matthew and the First Epistle of John, chapter three. Let us put these clearly before our mind.

In Matthew 25, following the parables of the wise and foolish virgins and the talents, which underscore our need to prepare ourselves for God's presence and to serve faithfully by using all God has given to us in order to sow greater love for him, the apostle gives us a vivid word picture of the Last Judgment. In this picture Jesus divides the "sheep from the goats"—those who are blessed from those condemned. The blessed are those who, when Jesus was hungry, fed him; when thirsty, gave him drink; when a stranger, welcomed him; when naked, clothed him; when sick, visited him; when in prison, came to him. "Truly," said Jesus, "as you did [these things] to one of the least of these my brethren, you did it to me" (25:40). Failure to prepare for him and failure to serve him is to be lost—*verfallen!* Even to forget cannot be used as an excuse. Here, loving God is to prepare for him and to serve him through the least of our brothers and sisters.

The apostle John makes it equally clear that the path to loving God and Jesus is through love of our neighbors. John also tells us that to love in this way is to abide in God and to have God abide in us, again underscoring the importance of learning to sense his presence. John says:

> By this we know love, that he laid down his life for us; and we ought to lay down our lives for the brethren. But if any one has the world's goods and sees his brother in need, yet closes his heart against him, how

does God's love abide in him? Little children, let us not
love in word or speech but in deed and in truth.

By this we shall know that we are of the truth, and
reassure our hearts before him whenever our hearts
condemn us; . . . And this is his commandment, that
we should believe in the name of his Son Jesus Christ
and love one another, just as he has commanded us.
All who keep his commandments abide in him, and he
in them. And by this we know that he abides in us, by
the Spirit which he has given us. (I John 3:16–20, 23–24)

Learning to abide with God is the goal of this third discipline of the human spirit, and *loving God by loving one another
is the trademark of this discipline* that we must explore further.

Loving God is a self-sacrificial act. It is the purpose for
which all our talk about possessing our self in order to give
our self was intended. Giving and sharing what we have
while we abide in God is an act of reciprocity like that from
child to parent; you give and share because you have been
given something in the first place. Our looks, our talent, our
wit were gifts to us, and our time, our food, and our wealth
are ours only to share with others. Loving, then, involves
sacrifice and reciprocity with God, and the end of loving is
to show the presence of God in our life—gratefully to declare in each moment of our lives Emmanuel, God with us.
But loving God, like attending and learning acts of refusal,
requires practice; it is a discipline for our spiritual improve-
ment.

Since loving God is a discipline, there are some forms of
behavior, some things that can be done, that will improve
such love. Three things should be remembered in loving
God: that loving God is an activity of contemplation and action, that it requires simple practices of the presence of God,
and that we must give attention to God through the compassion of Christ's way.

Contemplation and Action

One thing we must keep in mind about the discipline of
loving God is that our lives can be organized on more than

one level. Lanza del Vasto gave us a "perpetual exercise" whereby we reflect on our self in action. This, we saw, could be done while we were doing the things we were reflecting upon: thus two operations at once—two levels working together. Loving God in our ordinary lives requires a similar dual reflection and action. How might we envision this activity? It can most appropriately be understood as living our love of God through both contemplation and action. Contemplation and action are sister concepts to one another, like Mary and Martha.

Søren Kierkegaard once remarked, "If you want to show that your life is intended as service to God, then let it serve men, yet continually with the thought of God." Here, too, two operations—serving others while "continually" thinking of God. I may be teaching a class on an ordinary subject in philosophy without forgetting God. That does not mean the subject gets any religious interpretation, or that I verbalize my remembering God in any explicit fashion. I can express my being with God in every action in my life. In the case of my teaching, I express my being with God by my concern for the truth, by my zeal to communicate clearly, by my patience and understanding of students' questions and concerns, and by my awareness of bringing individual students from where they are to as close to a self-awareness of the truth as is possible.

When Paul said to pray without ceasing, we could easily respond, "But I'm not a monk or a hermit, I can't go around praying all the time; I've got business to attend to, a family to support, a child to raise." This is fair enough, but Paul is speaking of a manner of prayer that is more like living with a prayerful attitude (not, mind you, a pious attitude!). Brother Roger Schutz, prior of the community of Taizé in France, has urged us to become men and women of prayer, by which he means "seekers of communion"—*reaching toward* one another, as the apostle John said, while continually *reaching in* for the love of God. Our being a prayerful person and our loving God are inseparable. Fénelon remarked, "We cease to pray to God, as soon as we cease to love him" (*Selections*, p. 105).

Serving and praying with the thought of God and seeking communion with others can be seen as a form of the contemplative life. Contemplation is not the sole preserve of monks and hermits. Contemplation is reaching in for the love of God; it is, in the words of Thomas Merton, a "deepening" of our own "self-understanding, freedom, integrity and capacity to love" (*Contemplation in a World of Action*, p. 178). When such a deepening occurs, we are then free to love others.

A contemplative life, though not requiring withdrawal or isolation, does require solitude, and solitude requires some time and place of mind to recover one's deepest self. Solitude is an essential part of the discipline of loving God. It begins with the discipline of attention to this earthly life and draws us toward God's abiding love in us. This abiding love in us is the living Christ—the counselor and guide with us. Merton, again, characteristically said that the gift of solitude enables us to become persons who can give ourselves because we have a self to give. Furthermore, only as we possess our self can we find the living Christ in us and thus live his compassion freely (ibid., pp. 281f.).

Contemplation and action are a balance of living an interior and an exterior life in the spirit. Chrysostom (c. 345–407) reminds us that "nothing is so important as to keep an exact proportion between the interior source of virtue and the external practice of it." Such a balance between our interior life with God and our exterior earthly tasks is no great magical or counterfactual feat; we can organize on more than one level, and this is what makes possible our living in the spirit here and now! All of this is like learning to keep God before the "mind's eye" as we live our day-to-day lives.

Simple Practices of God's Presence

The disciplines for the human spirit described here are for beginners on the pilgrimage rather than part of an advanced contemplative spirituality. I have spoken little of the purgation of all desire, the annihilation of the self, meditation on the cross and passion of Christ, disinterested or pure love, rapture, and ecstasy. These may all be virtues for those very advanced in spiritual ways, but they are not for us here. Rather, I have been speaking of a contemplation available to all who wish to improve their life in the spirit and who will set out on this journey with us. Merton reformulates the term "contemplation" (ibid., p. 380) along lines given in the New Testament, so that each of us may aspire to be a contemplative person:

> Let us think of it in terms of knowing Jesus, being one of his disciples, being a member of the loving community which is called together in his merciful love, called to share his body and his blood together around the table of the Eucharistic banquet, called to realize in our love for one another and in our love for Jesus his presence in us.

With this notion of the contemplative spirit in mind, our ordinary life in the spirit might be instructed by this homely image given us by Brother Lawrence (1605–1691). He said, "I turn my little omelette in the pan for the love of God" (Barrois, p. 195). Of course, omelettes are not all, but this image may serve us better than a too-contrived methodological path or ways prescribed by the great mystics; we should save those for another day. Turning omelettes for the love of God, like doing your schoolwork with a view toward the love of God, is a way of equal value to practicing great austerities or bearing great crosses. In fact, these latter, as Père Grou warns, may create "illusions of self-love and [have] an effect of presumption" (*Spiritual Maxims*, p. 284). We must start simply. It is enough to remind ourselves that wherever we set out in this pilgrimage we will more than likely be led where we would rather not go, and for this we must prepare ourselves; the austerities and crosses will come soon enough. The Chambonnais in their simple life were beginners and by their devotion learned to walk in a way that outwardly was quite common and courageous. They were prepared, waiting at the door, for someone to knock. They had turned enough omelettes, in the right way, to know how to handle the Jewish child and the Vichy official when the door opened—even to face death, if that was what their love demanded.

Our struggles are human kitchen struggles, struggles in the workplace, with spouses and children, with our own anger and vices, with bureaucracies and powers who have forgotten God, with those harsh forces in the world that are indifferent to our virtues. In living these struggles every day, we must recognize our need for holy assistance and learn to abandon our worldly concerns to God—to cast our cares upon the Lord. This holy abandonment of cares is what Brother Lawrence often called "the practice of the presence of God." As we sense the spirit on our path and draw nearer to God, by his grace he draws near to us.

Loving God in the practice of his presence brings us back—it compels us back—to rethink all those ways of forgetting God. Now, in remembering God, we are given a new light and a new power to live within the secular surroundings of our life. For example: If we love God and abide with him, how different will be our attitude and our actions with regard to our self-importance and all our forms of self-fulfillment behavior; how different will be our manner of self-expression, now even abandonment, when we might otherwise seek to protect ourselves against harm or seek to harm others. If we love God and abide in him, we will remember Christ's death and not deny our own; we will live in the light of Christ's death and the spirit of his resurrection to build a hopeful and peaceful world for our children and heirs.

The practice of the presence of God itself is our calling as women and men of faith, as seekers and lovers. Roger Schutz put this practice simply in *This Day Belongs to God* when he said that "the Christian life is but a constant re-beginning, a return to grace every day, sometimes even every hour, through Him who, after each failure, pardons so that all things should be made new" (p. 29). In a call to individual Christians and to the churches (*Letter from Taizé*, February 1983), Brother Roger says that such new beginnings will lead to "a springtime of the heart." He includes these practices: placing confidence in God, reading Scripture, approaching the Eucharist with the simplicity of a child, forgiving one another, seeking communion with the oppressed and lonely, and making our homes and churches centers of hospitality.

Each discipline of the human spirit is about new beginnings; it is about renewing confidence in one's self as confidence is restored in God. It is about looking to God while refusing to yield to the moods of this world. It is about continuing the pilgrimage as a seeker, a lover, and a welcoming host. Because we are forgiven, even in all our forgetting, we can love. In this reciprocity with God waits "a springtime of the heart."

Fénelon, in addressing a young lady caught up with all the vanities of the court of Versailles, turns our attention to why the simple practices of recalling God's presence is so important to the discipline of loving God. He wrote to her in 1690 (*Spiritual Letters*, p. 25):

> It is only in looking steadfastly at God, and in loving him that we forget ourselves, that we free ourselves from this bauble which has dazzled us, and that we become accustomed to finding refuge in our smallness under the lofty majesty which engulfs everything. Love God, and you will be humble. Love God and you will no longer love yourself. Love God and you will love all that he wished you to love for love of him.

Loving God Through the Compassion of Christ's Way

There is always a lingering uncertainty because of our humanness that what we do, even our simple practices, may not be the consequence of our loving God. What certainty may we claim? How can we be sure that it is his abiding love that moves our heart? To approach this difficult question Simone Weil, again, gives us a helpful insight. In her *Notebooks* she says that when one gives sufficient attention to loving God then one is "constrained" to do God's will—God's will follows of its own accord. "The will of God," she says, "is that which one cannot but do when one has thought on him with sufficient attention and love" (p. 256). But how can this be so? And how are we to know what is *sufficient* attention and love?

Her notion of being constrained to do God's will by attention and love points us toward what it is like to act under another's power. If I constrain my daughter from plunging headlong into danger, she is not acting on her own power. I can also positively constrain her toward being kindly toward others by my example, encouragement, and judgment. So, too, because of the love Christ fixed on this world, on the woman of Samaria, on Zacchaeus, on Lazarus, on the blind and lame, they were under his constraint to go and spread the good news, to believe and sin no more.

The result of loving God is a new kind of constraint for us because it wrenches us away from ourselves. We are used to the constraints provided by our own acquired skills and energies, by our wealth and good luck, and by the authority and power accorded us by our place in society. These are all manifest to the degree that we are in charge of our own situations. These, of course, have nothing to do with our regard for God; they are secular constraints. Being constrained to do God's will by virtue of loving him orients us in a completely different manner. We are no longer in charge; we have a rope tied around our waists, pulling us toward God.

We have seen how fixing our attention, in the right way, on an object can enhance our love of God. Love itself, Weil says, is produced by fixing our attention on something real. When our love of God is pure, it moves through and beyond every object, material and human, that we encounter. The greater our attention and love of God is, the more we are constrained to do God's will. "To know that this man, who is cold and hungry, really exists as much as I do myself, and is really cold and hungry—that is enough, the rest follows of itself" (*Notebooks*, p. 449). To know another, that he or she exists, is the result of the right kind of attention with a view to the love of God. The ultimate pattern for doing God's will is to fix our attention on Christ as both God and human. God's constraint is shown as we take Christ as our model for God's abiding love.

Finally, let me give a brief theological account of this difficult point about being constrained by God's will through fixing our attention on Christ's way, rather than by attending to our own worldly way.

When Jesus proclaimed "I am the way, and the truth, and the life" (John 14:6), he was identifying himself *with God* and with his "new commandment" that we love one another as he had loved us (John 13:34, 35). *The way* is like the path of our pilgrimage; it leads the pilgrim to a spiritually noble condition *in life*, not to a heavenly place or particular far destination. *Following the way* is the manner by which we show our love of God, and this way involves our attentiveness to this created world and to our neighbor; it involves our growing to possess ourselves in order to be prepared to give ourselves out of compassion as ordinarily as we would seek our own self-interests. *The end of the way*, and therefore of loving God, is the formation of one's self in a very outward and public manner according to the "mind of Christ," as Paul said. Both our *personal sanctification* and the *redemption of the world* are bound up in our loving as Christ loved, here and now, in this present time, within the present human condition, however much suffering it may contain.

The way of the Christian pilgrimage must end in Christ, the living link to God. Our loving God is finally to dwell in Christ, and so to dwell is *to be changed* and so constrained as *to live his love* through compassion. To live Christ's love through compassion is to demonstrate that we are the benefactors of God's love. Simone Weil makes this point clearly when she says (*Science, Necessity, and the Love of God*, p. 191) that "only Christ's presence in a soul can put true compassion in it. But the Gospel reveals further that he who gives from true compassion gives Christ himself." In her 1942 "New York Notebook" (*First and Last Notebooks*, p. 103), she writes this about compassion:

> God is absent from the world, except in the existence in this world of those in whom His love is alive. There-

fore they ought to be present in the world through compassion. Their compassion is the visible presence of
God here below.

When we are lacking in compassion we make a violent separation between a creature and God.

Compassion is what spans this abyss. . . . Compassion is the rainbow.

"Compassion is the rainbow!" What a marvelous image—
a rainbow linking God's love to us through our compassion
to others. We live at one end of the rainbow, constrained to
love one another. This love is the enactment of a sacrament:
God's act of creation and incarnation, bringing into this
world, on the arc of a rainbow, the love of God that lies at
the other end.

As we increase in our attention to this earthly life and practice acts of refusal to compensate for the errant moods of this
world, we draw near to God. The consummating act is to regard God while we do these things and thus to call upon
Christ to dwell in our acts. To live in this way is to perform
the very sacrament of the Eucharist; it is to offer Christ as the
bread of life to others and turn life itself into a living sacrament. To regard God and to love in Christ's way are to live
one's life in *gratitude* and *compassion*.

CHAPTER TEN

SPIRITUAL PRESENCE

John of the Cross said that "the spirit must have an intimate sense that it is making a pilgrimage" and that the pilgrim's way is bringing the spirit "nearer the Divine sense" (p. 123). We have shown how a sense of God's presence is lived by loving God through the compassion of Christ's way. If we are to measure how intimate our sensing the spirit on a pilgrimage has been, we must be aware of how we are constrained in ever-increasing ways by God's will and not our own. There is a metamorphosis of the human spirit as we draw near to God and God transforms us into new creatures capable of reflecting the light of Christ. But before we envision that light as a halo surrounding our mortal heads, let us look at *the visible signs* of our journey's success, signs that we trust will remain with us even when we slip back into forgetting God and lose sight of the rainbow's far treasure.

A key visible sign of the increased constraint of God upon our lives that comes from our pilgrimage is *joy!* At the beginning of our journey, we could hardly imagine joy to be its benefit. Our beginning mood was sober, if not fearful. It appeared to be a long and arduous journey, one that we would rather not take. Because of our forgetfulness, we are reluctant to give up our self-governing constraints. Furthermore, we can legitimately fear new deceptions on a spiritual journey—forms of spiritual arrogance: illusions of self-love, false piety, and distancing ourself from the world. The apostle James, however, bids us forward with great vigor and says that we are assured by Christ that if we choose to go down this new path he will remain at our side and draw near to us. And if we avoid these new deceptions, then, as James says, we can "count it all joy!" James equates this joy with "fruit in holiness"—a holiness that has ripened into a form of spiritual presence in this world.

James uses the language of heartwork to show us the kinds of fruit we harvest from this holiness. The fruit, we are told, will counteract our "bitter jealousy" and our "selfish ambition" (James 3:14). We will be given *courage* to endure trial; *humility* to curb our arrogance and "tame the tongue" (3:8); *compassion* toward orphans, widows, and the poor; and *obedience* and *patience* while we "establish [our] hearts, for the coming of the Lord" (5:8). James also notes the joy of becoming a *peacemaker*, a sower of seeds to quell warring passions within ourselves and between one another.

Courage, humility, and compassion are fruits that emerge from all three disciplines on our pilgrimage. Being a peacemaker is a result of our acts of refusal when those acts are aimed at overcoming injustice and reconciling ourselves with victims of oppression and from the calm in our heart when we love God through Christ's way. It is primarily in the third discipline of loving God that we learn most of obedience and patience; it is in loving God that we "establish [our] hearts, for the coming of the Lord." All these virtues are strengthened in us as we practice the three disciplines of the human spirit.

Where some advanced contemplative patterns begin, our pilgrimage finds its end. There are *two active dispositions of the spirit* which, as we sense the presence of God, confirm our love of him; they are living signs that we have made progress toward establishing our hearts before him. They are the joyful harvest of our spiritual pilgrimage. These active dispositions of the spirit are to live within the present moment and take joy in it, and to live in communion with one another. We will conclude our pilgrimage with a brief look at each of these.

Live Joyfully in the Present Moment

One of the "greatest rules of the spiritual life," says Fénelon, is "to live within the present moment, without looking farther ahead" (*Spiritual Letters,* p. 112). Scripture testifies to this time and again. God provided the manna to the Israelites one day at a time, with amounts sufficient for the day. This is the message of Jesus in the Sermon on the Mount that we read so often but never really comprehend in our time: live each day for the day itself, without anxiety and worry. "Look at the birds of the air. . . . Consider the lilies of the field. . . . Let the day's own trouble be sufficient for the day" (Matt. 6:26, 28, 34). This, surely, is what Brother Roger meant by his remark that the Christian life is a "return to grace every day, sometimes even every hour."

Catherine of Siena (1347–1380), in a letter to a priest she called her "son," speaks of God lending us time in which to express our love. She said, "In lending time, and in time, God gives us many opportunities either to repent of our sins . . . or . . . to make us hate vice and love virtue" (Barrois, p. 119). This is very practical advice for loving God in the present moment *if* we take the time and seize the opportunities. The time in which we live is not ours; it is God's, lent to us so that we may use it to serve him. Thus to live within the present moment means we should work continually to remember God, to recall his presence. This we can do by recognizing all the ways God is absent from our lives, and in this recollection we will have taken a step toward practicing his presence.

Another important feature of living in the present moment and why we should take joy in it is the fact that life is provisional—we are provided for only for the time being. What may be of importance to us now may be of little consequence tomorrow. Thus care for the present while awaiting the future should be the manner of our life with God. This does not mean that we should never prepare for a future, but that whatever future there may be—and we know precious little what it *will* be—living with God *in this day* is our best way to prepare for and to have an effect upon the future. Living with God in this day provides us with *hope*.

Brother Roger, in *The Rule of Taizé*, likens provisional living to the spirit of the beatitudes, a spirit that sets "everything in the simple beauty of creation" and lives "in the gladness of today." This spirit prepares us to care for those contingencies of our earthly life when disaster strikes and people become lost and hungry, when tyranny terrorizes the human spirit, or when personal tragedy stalks at our doorstep.

Provisional living can also be *the demonstrable expression of Christ's redemption of our world.* This is hard to see, given the present chaos of our worldly life. But this chaos is of our own doing; it is the manifest making of a world without God. Were we to live *with* God in this present moment, we would be manifesting a different world—the peaceable kingdom! Given the world we do have, however, how can our living in the present with God move us toward a more peaceful future, a closer realization of God's kingdom?

To the degree that Christ dwells in us *as we show compassion* toward one another, Christ's redeeming power is at work creating a more humane and just world. To the degree that Christ dwells in us *as we show compassion* toward the afflicted and poor, we are actively thwarting hunger and oppression imposed on human beings by the principalities and powers of this world. To the degree that Christ dwells in us *as we show compassion* as peacemakers, we are engaged in making peace by struggling to revise the priorities of the worldly powers that threaten our annihilation and diminish our self-esteem. To the degree that Christ dwells in us *as we show compassion* toward and take joy in the life of each precious child of our planet, we are laying plans for a future that will survive us in spite of our human folly. This living with God in the present moment I called an *active* disposition of the spirit, and thus its effect in our history is relative *to the degree* that I dispose myself to remember God in these ways.

We have but one life to live in one time, and we must take our joy in it and no other. As we attend to our earthly life, in its beauty, and while we are present to other human beings, we should learn to enjoy them as the gifts they are.

There are simple joys, too: the smell of the lilacs in May, the laughter of children at play, the touch of a loved one knowing our needs, the warmth of the sun and the coolness of a breeze at sea, a meal shared among good friends. All the joy we feel comes down to us, says Teresa of Avila (1515–1582). "It is supernatural—quite outside our powers" (Hamilton, p. 51). Spiritual joy comes down to us; it is a form of "the laughter of the Divine love, of the Eternal Spirit which is in our spirits" (Peter Sterry, quoted in Wakefield, p. 68).

Because Christ's death and resurrection cast the world in a new light, we are called to joy in that light, to reflect it in our very presence in this world. To continue the passage from Schmemann quoted in Chapter Five, "This joy *transforms* all [our] human plans and programs, decisions and actions . . . [and through this joy] we see the true reality of the world and thus discover what we must do" (p. 113). This calls us to remember God in our forgetting, in the darkness of our time, and thus to recover the world, now in the new light—the light of the joy of Christ's presence with us.

Live in Communion with One Another

George MacDonald once wrote, "The one principle of hell is—'I am my own.' " This theme is not new to us. I have remarked a number of times that we cannot go it alone. Our life is a life in the world, but its joy depends on letting God rule us. What we can do in loving God moves us away from ourselves, but it does so only insofar as we love one another in the compassion that is Christ's way.

We cannot live alone and hope to do God's will. In the late fourth century, Saint Basil (330–379), in his *Rule*, attempted to restate a version of the Apostolic Church as a community of men and women living together in the world. He is said to have remarked once, "If you always live alone, whose feet will you wash?" It was fashionable in his time to become a solitary Christian, a hermit or desert monk, but Basil resisted this vigorously. To live in Christ's way there must be a community of believers. This has a clear precedent in the Scripture, and its sharpest image is that of Pentecost, where

the Holy Spirit filled the heart of thousands from many nations with many tongues and gave them unique powers for
discernment of God's spirit. Luke writes that they received
God's word and were baptized: "And they devoted themselves to the apostles' teaching and fellowship, to the breaking of bread and the prayers" (Acts 2:42). All alienation that
may have been characteristic of their side-by-sideness as they
started listening to Peter's message was broken down by
God's grace. Formed into cell-like units, the people

> were together and had all things in common; and they
> sold their possessions and goods and distributed them
> to all, as any had need. And day by day, attending the
> temple together and breaking bread in their homes,
> they partook of food with glad and generous hearts,
> praising God and having favor with all the people.
> (Acts 2:44–47, also see Acts 4:32–35)

Community is a fruit of our communion with God. The
practice of God's presence is best done within human community, centered around a few sacred and simple reminders: the reading of God's word in Scripture, the breaking of
bread (the Eucharist), fellowship in prayer and song, and
sharing of food with glad and generous hearts. As these are
shared in common and flow outward toward the world, the
holiness of the people of God is shown to all and Christ's redeeming power is once again visibly at work.

To have communion with one another is to be a person of
community. To abide with God and he with us means watch-
ing on behalf of others: to watch and listen for the deceptions of our time about our importance and our power, about
denying death while producing its purest instruments. It
means gathering together: gathering together the joys and
hopes of all people, as well as their anxieties and sufferings.
To have communion means patiently to weave ties of love
between all brothers and sisters: ties of reconciliation, forgiveness, and fellowship.

A beloved student of mine once expressed this meaning of
communion as community very simply as "the willingness to

live beyond oneself—in commitment to a discipline, a belief, and to others . . . to think of oneself less and others more." To have such a disposition to communion is a natural outcome of our pilgrimage. From our ordinary forgetfulness to our individual struggles with prayer and attention and through our declarations of spiritual independence, we are moved toward remembering God and dependence upon him and thus toward a common life in the spirit.

EPILOGUE

Spiritual presence is a special way of being in the world with God—it is the end of our pilgrimage route. Spiritual presence is a way of being present to oneself in this earthly life; it embraces all the active dispositions of the spirit and reflects living with an established heart in the presence of God.

In 1903, Tolstoy wrote a brief tale that illustrates this concept of spiritual presence. The tale, "Three Questions," begins:

> It once occurred to a certain king, that if he always knew the right time to begin everything; if he knew who were the right people to listen to and whom to avoid; and, above all, if he always knew what was the most important thing to do, he would never fail in anything he might undertake.

With these three things posed as questions, the king began his search for the right answers. He offered a great reward and summoned to his court learned men and women. Priests and prophets, warriors and doctors, lords and counselors, all answered his questions differently, so the king dismissed them. Hearing of a wise hermit who never left the forest and only received common folk, the king put on simple clothes and sought out the hermit.

When the king found the hermit, he was digging in front of his hut preparing to plant seeds. The hermit was frail and breathed heavily. The king approached the hermit with his three questions. The hermit said nothing and went on digging. The king, recognizing the hermit's fatigue, asked to help with digging. They dug, alternating rest, until sunset.

Suddenly a wounded man came running toward them. "The man held his hands pressed against his stomach, and blood was flowing from under them." The stranger fainted and fell before the king. The king and the hermit immediately dressed his wounds and laid him in the hermit's hut. The king kept watch over him and fell asleep himself. When the king awoke at sunrise, the stranger was "gazing intently at him with shining eyes." "Forgive me!" said the man to the king. The king replied, "I do not know you, and have nothing to forgive you for." The stranger said that he knew the king and had set an ambush in the woods to kill the king and avenge his brother's death, who had been sentenced by the king. But on the way, the king's bodyguards recognized him as the king's enemy and wounded him and he fled into the woods. He then happened upon the king and the hermit. The king was happy to have made peace with an enemy so easily and forgave the stranger and restored to him his brother's property.

Meanwhile, outside, the hermit was sowing seeds in the freshly dug beds. The king, still wishing an answer to his three questions, approached the hermit once more and said, "For the last time, I pray you to answer my questions, wise man." Tolstoy ends his tale with this exchange:

"You have already been answered!" said the hermit, still crouching on his thin legs, and looking up at the King, who stood before him.

"How answered? What do you mean" asked the King.

"Do you not see," replied the hermit. "If you had not pitied my weakness yesterday and had not dug these beds for me, but had gone your way, that man would have attacked you and you would have repented of not having stayed with me. So the most important time was when you were digging the beds; and I was the most important man; and to do me good was your most important business. Afterwards, when that man ran to us, the most important time was when you were attending to him, for if you had not bound up his wounds he would have died without having made peace with you. So he was the most important man, and what you did for him was your most important business. Remember then: there is only one time that is important—Now! It is the most important time because it is the only time when we have any power. The most necessary man is he with whom you are, for no man knows whether he will ever have dealings with any one else: and the most important affair is, to do him good, because for that purpose alone was man sent into this life!"

To be present to one another, here and now, is to be present to God. If we begin to sense God's spirit in us, we will remember him and, in this remembrance, desire to love him. This desire sets us on the pilgrim's path; and with a genuine effort of the human spirit, all else will follow of itself.

LIST OF WORKS CITED

Allen, Diogenes. *The Traces of God.* Cowley Publications, 1981.

Augustine of Hippo. *Confessions.* Tr. by R. S. Pine-Coffin. Penguin Books, 1961.

Barrois, Georges A. (ed.). *Pathways of the Inner Life: An Anthology of Christian Spirituality.* Bobbs-Merrill Co., 1957.

Berrigan, Daniel. *Ten Commandments for the Long Haul.* Abingdon Press, 1981.

Bunyan, John. *The Pilgrim's Progress.* New American Library of World Literature (Signet Classic), 1964.

Dostoyevsky, Fyodor. *The Brothers Karamazov.* Random House (Vintage Books), 1955.

Fénelon, François. *Selections from the Writings of Fénelon.* Boston: Hilliard, Gray, Little, and Wilkins, 1831.

————. *Spiritual Letters of Fénelon.* Tr. by Mildred W. Stillman. Cornwall-on-Hudson, N.Y.: Idlewild Press, 1945.

Francis de Sales. *Introduction to the Devout Life.* Tr. by John K. Ryan. Harper & Row (Harper Torchbooks), 1966.

Gass, William H. *Fiction and the Figures of Life.* Alfred A. Knopf, 1970.

Grou, Jean Nicolas. *Spiritual Maxims.* London: Burns & Oates, 1961.

Hallie, Philip P. *Lest Innocent Blood Be Shed: The Story of the Village of Le Chambon and How Goodness Happened There.* Harper & Row, 1979.

Hamilton, Elizabeth (ed.). *Servants of Love: The Spirituality of Teresa of Avila.* London: Darton, Longman & Todd, 1975.

John of the Cross. *Dark Night of the Soul.* Tr. by E. Allison Peers. Doubleday & Co. (Image Books), 1959.

Kierkegaard, Søren. *Parables of Kierkegaard.* Ed. by Thomas C. Oden. Princeton University Press, 1978.

Kushner, Harold S. *When Bad Things Happen to Good People.* Schocken Books, 1981.

Lanza del Vasto, Joseph J. *Make Straight the Way of the Lord.* Tr. by Jean Sidgwick. Alfred A. Knopf, 1974.

————. *Principles and Precepts of the Return to the Obvious.* Schocken Books, 1974.

Lawrence, Brother (Nicholas Hermann). *The Practice of the Presence of God.* Fleming H. Revell Co., 1958.

Merton, Thomas. *Contemplation in a World of Action.* Doubleday & Co. (Image Books), 1973.

————. *Life and Solitude* [sound recordings]. Chappaqua, N.Y., Electronic Paperbacks, n.d. Taped from lectures at Gethsemani, Kentucky, 1951–1965.

Nouwen, Henri J. M. *The Living Reminder: Service and Prayer in Memory of Jesus Christ.* Seabury Press, 1977.

O'Connor, Flannery. *The Habit of Being: Letters.* Ed. by Sally Fitzgerald. Farrar, Straus, 1979.

Plato. *The Last Days of Socrates.* Tr. by Hugh Tredennick. Penguin Books, 1969.

Schell, Jonathan. *The Fate of the Earth.* Alfred A. Knopf, 1982.

Schmemann, Alexander. *For the Life of the World: Sacraments and Orthodoxy.* New York: St. Vladimir's Seminary Press, 1973.

Schutz, Roger. *The Rule of Taizé.* Taizé, France: Les Presses de Taizé, 1968.

————. *This Day Belongs to God.* London: Faith Press, 1961.

Steere, Douglas V. *On Beginning from Within.* Harper & Brothers, 1943.

Tolstoy, Leo. *The Death of Ivan Ilych and Other Stories.* Tr. by Aylmer Maude. New American Library of World Literature (Signet Classic), 1960.

————. *Twenty-Three Tales.* London: Henry Frowde, Oxford University Press, 1906.

Turner, Victor and Edith. *Image and Pilgrimage in Christian Culture.* Columbia University Press, 1978.

Wakefield, Gordon S. (ed.). *The Westminster Dictionary of Christian Spirituality.* Westminster Press, 1983.

Weil, Simone. *First and Last Notebooks.* Tr. by Richard Rees. London: Oxford University Press, 1970.

————. *Gravity and Grace.* Tr. by Emma Craufurd. London: Routledge and Kegan Paul, 1963.

————. *The Iliad or the Poem of Force.* Wallingford, Pa.: Pendle Hill Pamphlet no. 91, 1981.

————. *The Notebooks of Simone Weil.* 2 vols. London: Routledge and Kegan Paul, 1976.

————. *On Science, Necessity, and the Love of God.* London: Oxford University Press, 1968.

————. *The Simone Weil Reader.* Ed. by George A. Panichas. David McKay Co., 1977.

————. *Two Moral Essays: Human Personality and On Human Obligations.* Wallingford, Pa.: Pendle Hill Pamphlet no. 240, 1981.

————. *Waiting for God.* Tr. by Emma Craufurd. Harper & Row (Colophon Books), 1973.

Wittgenstein, Ludwig. *Culture and Value.* Ed. by G. H. von Wright, tr. by Peter Winch. University of Chicago Press, 1980.

Wolf, Christa. *A Model Childhood.* Tr. by Ursule Molinaro and Hedwig Rappolt. Farrar, Straus & Giroux, 1980.